EVERYTHING THAT RISES
MUST CONVERGE

A.T.L.

AMERICAN THEATER IN LITERATURE

Advisory Board

Gordon Davidson
Kenward Elmslie
David Henry Hwang
Tony Kushner
Jerome Lawrence
Richard Nelson
Eric Overmyer
Katherine Owens
Suzan-Lori Parks
Carey Perloff
Peter Sellars
Fiona Templeton
Mac Wellman

Douglas Messerli, *Publisher*

• **JOHN JESURUN**

Everything That Rises Must Converge

SUN & MOON PRESS
LOS ANGELES • 1997

Sun & Moon Press
A Program of The Contemporary Arts Educational Project, Inc.
a nonprofit corporation
6026 Wilshire Boulevard, Los Angeles, California 90036
website: http://www.sunmoon.com

First Sun & Moon Press edition 1997
10 9 8 7 6 5 4 3 2 1
©1997, 1990 by John Jesurun
All rights reserved

CAUTION: Professionals and amateurs are hereby warned that this work is fully protected under the copyright laws of all jurisdictions of the world and that all rights in this work (professional, amateur or otherwise), including but not limited to motion picture, television, recitation, performance, public reading, radio broadcast, and translation rights, are strictly reserved. Any presentation or other use of this work for any purpose other than private reading thereof requires advance permission, payment of a royalty and other terms and conditions to be secured in writing from John Jesurun, c/o Sun & Moon Press.

This book was made possible, in part, through contributions to The Contemporary Arts Educational Project, Inc., a nonprofit corporation, and through a grant from the National Endowment for the Arts (Heritage and Preservation).

NATIONAL
ENDOWMENT
FOR THE
ARTS

Cover: Anselm Kiefer, *Father, Son, Holy Ghost* (1973)
Design: Katie Messborn
Typography: Guy Bennett

LIBRARY OF CONGRESS CATALOGING IN PUBLICATION DATA
Jesurun, John
Everything That Rises Must Converge
p. cm (Sun & Moon Classics: 116/ATL-American Theater in Literature)
ISBN: 1-557713-053-1
I. Title. II. Author
811'.54—dc20

Printed in the United States of America on acid-free paper.

Without limiting the rights under copyright reserved here, no part of this publication may be reproduced, stored in or introduced into a retrieval system, or transmitted, in any form or by any means (electronic, mechanical, photocopying, recording or otherwise), without the prior written permission of both the copyright owner and the above publisher of the book.

To Ritsaert ten Cate
and Ellen Stewart

Everything That Rises Must Converge was co-produced and presented in 1990 by: The Walker Arts Center, Minneapolis, Minnesota; The Wexner Center For Visual Arts, Columbus, Ohio; The Kitchen, New York City; The Mickery Theater, Amsterdam, Netherlands; Maubeuge International Theater Festival, Maubeuge, France; De Singel Theater, Antwerp, Belgium; The Vienna Festival, Vienna, Austria and the Spoleto Festival, USA, Charleston, South Carolina. It premiered on January 31, 1990 at the Walker Arts Center, Minneapolis.

It was performed by:

Oscar de la Fé Colón	OSCAR
Joe Murphy	JOE
Susanne Strenger	MRS PEABODY
Larry Tighe	YOUR HIGHNESS
Michael Tighe	FREDDIE MAYFIELD
Sanghi Wagner	THE QUEEN
Phyllis Young	PHYLLIS
On video:	
Jonathan Del Arco	LAGRIMAS
Jane Smith	

Directed and designed by John Jesurun; lighting design by Jeff Nash; technical director/production manager, Dayton Taylor; cameras, Barrett Schumacher, David Tumblety, Dayton Taylor, Catherine Gore.

Excerpted material:

"La Relacion." Official report by Cabeza de Vaca to Charles v King of Spain, 154

"Sunshine, Lollipops and Roses" (Hamlisch-Heimel)

"Polly Von" Traditional folk song, (Yarrow, Stookey, Travers)

"Share Your Love With Me" [Al Braggs-Deadric Malone]

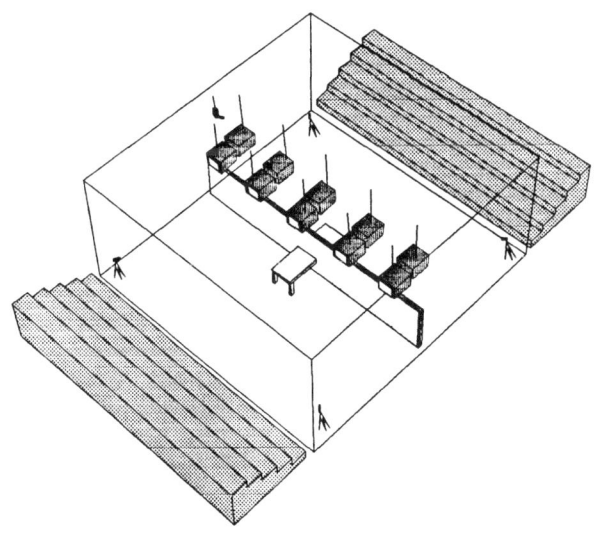

The stage, actors and audience are divided by a wall nine feet high and up to forty feet wide depending on the playing space. One side is painted black and the other white. There is a rectangular table at the center on each side of the wall. At times the wall rotates on its center vertical axis revealing the actors to the opposite side. The seven live actors form two teams, one on either side of the wall. They interact with those on the other side through live video and wireless microphones. Four camera operators positioned on each of the corners of the playing area capture the images of the actors. These images appear live on ten monitors suspended above the wall. In addition to these perspectives, video switching allows the view of a remote control camera with a bird's eye view of the stage and the two prerecorded actors to change in a variety of different configurations within the bank of monitors.

On one side of the wall are:
>THE QUEEN
>*Her Interpreters:*
>FREDDIE MAYFIELD, JOE *and* MRS PEABODY

On the other side are:
>**YOUR HIGHNESS**
>*His Interpreters:*
>**OSCAR** *and* **PHYLLIS**

On video only:
>*LAGRIMAS*

- **RESTRICTIVE PROVISIONS**

OSCAR: [*In Spanish*] I have a gift for you, a new world, the gift of poison.
MRS PEABODY: [*Repeats in German*]
OSCAR: Your language is powerful, disgusting and I have the right to choose the questions and revise the answers. Always I retain that right. It is my right by right of conquest. I've told you that before.
MRS PEABODY: [*Repeats in German*]
THE QUEEN: I demand it.
MRS PEABODY: [*Repeats in German*]
OSCAR: [*Repeats in Spanish*]
PHYLLIS: I demand it.
THE QUEEN: I will be asked no questions about my private life, views or activities.
MRS PEABODY: [*Repeats in German*]
OSCAR: [*Repeats in Spanish*]
PHYLLIS: I will be asked no questions about my private life, views or activities.
JOE: No extraneous material will be removed.
THE QUEEN: You're a hack, don't touch.
JOE: But we've made contact.
THE QUEEN: Counter proposal.
PHYLLIS: Abdication.
MRS PEABODY: Black balled, banished, vanished.
FREDDIE MAYFIELD: Olvidated, guernicated.
JOE: We have made contact.
OSCAR: Take it with a grain of pepper or gunpowder.
THE QUEEN: OK, we've made contact.

YOUR HIGHNESS: Serve the milk and rice!
JOE: I have made contact.
THE QUEEN: With who, with what?
JOE: My work is extensive in that area. You will have to trust me.

- **RE-ENTRY**

YOUR HIGHNESS: Prepare for reentry.
THE QUEEN: What time is the convocation?
MRS PEABODY: Just enough time to finish this glass of wine.
JOE: It begins at three.
PHYLLIS: Are you talking to me?
YOUR HIGHNESS: Yes.
THE QUEEN: Then get me my notes and keep going.
OSCAR: Get my notebook.
THE QUEEN: Have you prepared a retaliatory response?
MRS PEABODY: Get my notebook.
FREDDIE MAYFIELD: Are you listening to me?
MRS PEABODY: Yes.
YOUR HIGHNESS: Have you prepared a response?
JOE: Yes.
THE QUEEN: It's in my head I'll dictate it in an hour.
PHYLLIS: The convocation is in ten minutes.
JOE: I know that.
FREDDIE MAYFIELD: What was that surge?
MRS PEABODY: Check the circuit breaker.
OSCAR: I'm the only one you can trust with the switch, give it to me.
THE QUEEN: Are you happy here?
JOE: No.
THE QUEEN: Carry on then.
MRS PEABODY: Yes, your highness.
OSCAR: Don't call me that.
YOUR HIGHNESS: What are your sentiments about this?

OSCAR: I don't have any.

THE QUEEN: You are paid to have sentiments and you will tell me them.

JOE: I have precautionary presentiments.

YOUR HIGHNESS: Out with them.

PHYLLIS: No.

THE QUEEN: They are clandestine, reckless, provocative.

YOUR HIGHNESS: I want you to return their message.

FREDDIE MAYFIELD: Oh dear, it's after 12. Time to cut out.

PHYLLIS: Prepare for reentry and send this.

YOUR HIGHNESS: What about the 12:30 feed?

MRS PEABODY: Send it out without an answer as if we never read it.

OSCAR: Why would we do that?

FREDDIE MAYFIELD: Don't know yet but seems like a good move.

PHYLLIS: It's stupid.

YOUR HIGHNESS: It doesn't mean anything.

THE QUEEN: It is precisely because it doesn't mean anything that they will imagine it does and become confused.

JOE: We'll just keep winging until something appears on the horizon and then maybe we'll do that if it appears to create a presentiment.

MRS PEABODY: Then let it fly.

FREDDIE MAYFIELD: We can deal with the something, I can't think of the word.

OSCAR: You don't even know what you're doing.

FREDDIE MAYFIELD: They don't even know what they're doing.

PHYLLIS: What are they doing?
YOUR HIGHNESS: The same thing we are.
THE QUEEN: Do you like to dance?
JOE: Yes.
YOUR HIGHNESS: Where is my book?
THE QUEEN: Shall we dance later?
JOE: Sure.
MRS PEABODY: How is the disco?
OSCAR: Still pumping.
FREDDIE MAYFIELD: I hate this job.
PHYLLIS: You're such a sad sack!
YOUR HIGHNESS: I know that!
JOE: Why are you so sad?
THE QUEEN: Don't touch me.
JOE: I haven't yet have I?
MRS PEABODY: You're not allowed.
OSCAR: No.
JOE: When can I?
THE QUEEN: Perhaps after the convocation if it's a success.
JOE: Don't get your hopes up.
MRS PEABODY: Why is this space all empty?
OSCAR: I don't know.
FREDDIE MAYFIELD: Wasn't there a presentiment in here originally?
PHYLLIS: No.
YOUR HIGHNESS: Yes there was, I saw it myself.
THE QUEEN: Some sort of space oddity.
JOE: It hasn't slipped out on the feed has it?
MRS PEABODY: What was the presentiment? Return it to its place.

OSCAR: I can't find it anywhere.//
FREDDIE MAYFIELD: We cannot leave the space empty.
PHYLLIS: That's not what was there.
YOUR HIGHNESS: What was there?
THE QUEEN: You dictated it yourself.
JOE: Why does the space keep coming up empty?
THE QUEEN: Please don't touch me, just give me my shoe when I ask for it!
JOE: Yes your highness.
YOUR HIGHNESS: I asked you to please not call me that! Don't call me anything!
JOE: Fine.
THE QUEEN: Now, could you please give me that shoe and find the missing segment to that directive.
JOE: Can't you remember it?
MRS PEABODY: You wrote it down so I wouldn't have to remember it.
OSCAR: The intersection we're trying to create is totally screwed because there's a hole in it.
FREDDIE MAYFIELD: It's been misplaced.
THE QUEEN: The shoe.
PHYLLIS: Why does it keep coming up empty?
THE QUEEN: And please just the shoe I said. I can't afford to have a relationship with an inferior, you do understand?
YOUR HIGHNESS: How is the DJ?
THE QUEEN: Spinning.
JOE: Spoiled.
THE QUEEN: Invite him for dinner.
JOE: What for?
THE QUEEN: I'd like to discuss music.

YOUR HIGHNESS: And then maybe we'll dance later.

MRS PEABODY: What could he tell you that you would want to know?

OSCAR: Run down what we've said.

FREDDIE MAYFIELD: Erase the last two lines, cancel them completely and send the rest through the remote wire so they can read it.

PHYLLIS: Why would they want to read it?

YOUR HIGHNESS: I'm interested to see what they do with it when it gets spun through their code.

THE QUEEN: OK.

JOE: Where is Lagrimas?

MRS PEABODY: Three floors above us tying this up.

OSCAR: Only the machine is to get a hold of this, put him out to lunch for the moment.

FREDDIE MAYFIELD: Lagrimas, lunch! Can you hear me?

YOUR HIGHNESS: What time is my piano lesson?

PHYLLIS: After the convocation.

THE QUEEN: Then the French lesson.

JOE: Who?

MRS PEABODY: Never mind.

OSCAR: Hello, who's this?

FREDDIE MAYFIELD: I don't know, don't bother me.

PHYLLIS: You've inverted the terminologies, misplaced the original segment.

YOUR HIGHNESS: Retranslate it again and then translate it backwards and forwards a few times to insure the idiot proof.

THE QUEEN: Shut up and get out of here.

JOE: Look at my face.

MRS PEABODY: Look at my face, I said.

OSCAR: What do you see?
FREDDIE MAYFIELD: Nothing.
PHYLLIS: I don't see anything either.
YOUR HIGHNESS: What do you see in my face?
THE QUEEN: And get that smoldering blanket out of my bedroom.
JOE: What is it?
THE QUEEN: Go.
MRS PEABODY: What will we charge them with?
OSCAR: Premeditation and malfeasance.
FREDDIE MAYFIELD: Double or nothing.
PHYLLIS: That's fine.
YOUR HIGHNESS: I don't want to be disturbed but don't argue to the point of insult.
THE QUEEN: Why not?
JOE: You know better than I do.
MRS PEABODY: The rupture, the lesion, the tear, the rip.
OSCAR: You know what I'm talking about.
FREDDIE MAYFIELD: The rat and mouse game.
THE QUEEN: Please take off my shoe, just the shoe please, left.
PHYLLIS: One of them has turned into some kind of grotesque alcoholic.
YOUR HIGHNESS: Like Bette Davis?
THE QUEEN: Oh, how awful.
JOE: Sniffling and sniggering their way from convocation to convocation.
THE QUEEN: Don't touch.
MRS PEABODY: Just the shoe.
OSCAR: We're not talking about that now.
FREDDIE MAYFIELD: Then what are we talking about?

PHYLLIS: The 11:30 feed.
YOUR HIGHNESS: It's 12:30, it's already out.
THE QUEEN: It's too late to do anything.
JOE: Can we issue a retraction?
MRS PEABODY: It's not retractable.
OSCAR: Why not? What about the 12:30 feed?
FREDDIE MAYFIELD: It's going out now.
PHYLLIS: Then the 10:00.
YOUR HIGHNESS: You can't throw it out and pull it in, no one will believe it!
THE QUEEN: Do it anyway. Put it on the second level.
JOE: Does anyone know what we're saying?
MRS PEABODY: Whatever it is, it has real killing power. They can't think of an answer.
OSCAR: Can you hear me?
FREDDIE MAYFIELD: I said it couldn't kill a fly.
PHYLLIS: First witness.
YOUR HIGHNESS: Call Mr. Somebody what was his name?
THE QUEEN: He's on fire with so much to confess.
JOE: Caught inflagrante.
MRS PEABODY: Is he ready?
OSCAR: So what else is new?
FREDDIE MAYFIELD: He has infiltrated our corridor.
PHYLLIS: Coordinator.
YOUR HIGHNESS: Don't believe them. They've all slept with each other but they don't realize it yet.
THE QUEEN: Oh, that's nothing, they've all informed on each other separately.
JOE: They'll find out and no one will mind.
THE QUEEN: Not that shoe.

MRS PEABODY: Steady now, hold back the dogs.
OSCAR: Steady now, easy now, hold back the dogs.
FREDDIE MAYFIELD: Dogs?
PHYLLIS: The dogs. Our dogs?
YOUR HIGHNESS: Yes, our dogs. Hold them back. Steady now, easy now, hold them back.
THE QUEEN: It's another one of their epileptic, canine diversions.
JOE: Steady now.
OSCAR: What a jerk.
MRS PEABODY: What are they saying?
THE QUEEN: I'll cut them down I'll slash them to pieces. I'll find a part of them they didn't know they had.
OSCAR: [SPANISH]
YOUR HIGHNESS: Are they angry?
PHYLLIS: It's the coordinator.
YOUR HIGHNESS: And where is he?
THE QUEEN: He's having barbeque across the border.
JOE: Enchiladas and ribs.
MRS PEABODY: 6:00 feed.
OSCAR: My rib hurts.
THE QUEEN: Give me more pills.
PHYLLIS: Nose clogged?
YOUR HIGHNESS: Now what?
THE QUEEN: How dare you attempt an eclipse on the black dahlia.
FREDDIE MAYFIELD: Put that shoe back.
OSCAR: What is the projection?
JOE: Mudslide.
YOUR HIGHNESS: Reject that.
THE QUEEN: Did they refund that?

YOUR HIGHNESS: I didn't ask for a retraction.
THE QUEEN: I asked for a subtraction, not a retraction.
FREDDIE MAYFIELD: Operator?
OSCAR: I sense a mistake, a tiny puny mistake that will bring us down.
FREDDIE MAYFIELD: Snowballing into a landslide.
THE QUEEN: What mistake?
JOE: There is no mistake.
MRS PEABODY: Don't ask him, he's just a crummy postal worker.
OSCAR: Where is the finance director?
FREDDIE MAYFIELD: Dead.
PHYLLIS: How did that happen?
YOUR HIGHNESS: He was removed.
THE QUEEN: I didn't know that.
JOE: Who removed him?
MRS PEABODY: It had to be done.
OSCAR: Don't give me that bullyshit.
FREDDIE MAYFIELD: Who confounded this?
PHYLLIS: We rejected his prodigal son act.
YOUR HIGHNESS: What's the final count?
THE QUEEN: The registration is incorrect.
JOE: It ain't.
MRS PEABODY: What's the reaction?
OSCAR: Shrill, harsh.
FREDDIE MAYFIELD: Strategy?
PHYLLIS: She's been elected queen.
YOUR HIGHNESS: Elected by the...
THE QUEEN: The what?
JOE: The council of selectors.
MRS PEABODY: The electrocutors of...

OSCAR: Put a point on my pencil.

FREDDIE MAYFIELD: Sharpen.

PHYLLIS: Beat it into a sword and don't poke yourself.

JOE: More projectiles.

YOUR HIGHNESS: You are a criminal and an asswipe and I will not have this here in my room! Close the door, they don't have to hear this.

MRS PEABODY: Isn't this your client?

OSCAR: No he is not.

FREDDIE MAYFIELD: Then whose client is he?

PHYLLIS: I thought he was yours.

YOUR HIGHNESS: I was under the impression he was yours.

THE QUEEN: Whose is this man?

JOE: Who does he belong to?

MRS PEABODY: An umbrella organization of all of us under which he is held.

OSCAR: He belongs to all of us, not just one.

FREDDIE MAYFIELD: We all share equal responsibility in holding the umbrella.

THE QUEEN: Are you buckin' me?

MRS PEABODY: What do you mean buckin'?

YOUR HIGHNESS: What does he mean buckin'?

MRS PEABODY: [*German*]

OSCAR: [*Spanish*]

FREDDIE MAYFIELD: Bucking, a bucking bronco.

THE QUEEN: You buckin' me.

JOE: What happened to your eye?

FREDDIE MAYFIELD: Nothing.

PHYLLIS: What happened to your eye?

MRS PEABODY: What is happening to your eye?

YOUR HIGHNESS: You buckin' me!
JOE: We don't have maneuvering room.
YOUR HIGHNESS: But you're so thin.
OSCAR: Haven't you been eating well?
PHYLLIS: Their screwball intelligencia is bucking their own coordinator.
MRS PEABODY: Can I interrupt?
OSCAR: No.
FREDDIE MAYFIELD: Can I interrupt?
PHYLLIS: Can I ask a question?
YOUR HIGHNESS: The implementation segment is fragments.
THE QUEEN: Who dropped it?
JOE: Well, so what.
MRS PEABODY: What do you want?
OSCAR: We don't want.
FREDDIE MAYFIELD: We don't want.
PHYLLIS: Who dropped it?
YOUR HIGHNESS: No we don't, don't want.
THE QUEEN: Don't want.
JOE: Don't want what?
MRS PEABODY: Who don't want?
THE QUEEN: Get out of my house!
YOUR HIGHNESS: Get my air dresser, it stinks in here.
OSCAR: The ballroom….
THE QUEEN: The ballroom what?
JOE: Has exploded, the chandelier has rotated into the floor.
MRS PEABODY: Oh my dear darling, I'm so sorry.
OSCAR: What are you sorry about?
FREDDIE MAYFIELD: I loved that chandelier.

THE QUEEN: It was my chandelier, you aren't allowed to love it.

PHYLLIS: Something about a chandelier.

JOE: Don't accept, it's one of his menopausal manias.

YOUR HIGHNESS: He's an egghead.

THE QUEEN: You're such an egghead.

PHYLLIS: Don't insult them.

YOUR HIGHNESS: You're pushing all the wrong buttons.

MRS PEABODY: Are you afraid?

THE QUEEN: You have to understand, it's a personal moment of stupidity and it's all mine.

YOUR HIGHNESS: Shut him up!

THE QUEEN: And shut that disco up! Shut it down!

OSCAR: What has gone wrong there?

FREDDIE MAYFIELD: Almost everything.

PHYLLIS: The hostility let loose. Released itself into the atmosphere and we can't snatch it back.

YOUR HIGHNESS: The insurgency.

THE QUEEN: I think we have to wrap it up now.

JOE: Then wrap the damn thing up. I don't care. I could give a fuck!

MRS PEABODY: Something very big has gone down the drain.

OSCAR: Why do you say those things?

FREDDIE MAYFIELD: The night stalker is preparing for the hemorrhage.

PHYLLIS: A shining white trick, a political hunchback. Whether deliberately or not it is just one and it's not over till it's over.

YOUR HIGHNESS: It's over and it is over.

THE QUEEN: You've been cancelled, I'm sorry to say.

JOE: Now is that fully automatic?
MRS PEABODY: Automatically.
YOUR HIGHNESS: Book me into the motel.
OSCAR: Single or double?
FREDDIE MAYFIELD: Double or nothing.
THE QUEEN: Where are my pain killers?
PHYLLIS: We've booked him into a motel, he's descended into some kind of unparalleled anxiety.
JOE: Over what?
YOUR HIGHNESS: Reject that, it's an inversion.
MRS PEABODY: Into what?
YOUR HIGHNESS: You know what and I know what and we all know what.
THE QUEEN: We reject it and we're sending it back unread and unsigned. Resignify the feedback.
MRS PEABODY: Without a signifier?
YOUR HIGHNESS: Well, we won't accept it. Shut down the receiver.
OSCAR: Too late.
THE QUEEN: Send it out again.
FREDDIE MAYFIELD: Too late, they've shut down their receiver and rejected it.
YOUR HIGHNESS: So now we've got it and we don't want it.
THE QUEEN: And we know they don't want it.
OSCAR: Send it somewhere else.
YOUR HIGHNESS: To the moon Alice, to the moon!
MRS PEABODY: The power is failing.
PHYLLIS: He's so strung out we had to book him into a motel.
YOUR HIGHNESS: The little green men are coming.

JOE: You don't have to shout.
MRS PEABODY: How are things in the disco?
OSCAR: Everyone's dead in there.
FREDDIE MAYFIELD: Smothered in its own ash.
PHYLLIS: A total wipe.
YOUR HIGHNESS: That little whore.
THE QUEEN: I have a nosebleed again.
FREDDIE MAYFIELD: I am not a little whore!
OSCAR: It's the altitude.
YOUR HIGHNESS: Can't you bring this crate down a little bit lower?
MRS PEABODY: Do you always have to fly so damn high?
PHYLLIS: We've got to go high and stay high.
YOUR HIGHNESS: I'm getting dizzy I'm telling you.
THE QUEEN: Please go lower, my ears!
YOUR HIGHNESS: Lower, please!
THE QUEEN: Please!
JOE: Now, what's the next sentence?
OSCAR: [*Spanish*]
YOUR HIGHNESS: Transfer.
JOE: We've saturated the line, satisfied?
THE QUEEN: It's too hard to swallow. Again please.
OSCAR: She's drifting again, please, number 4.
MRS PEABODY: How many times do we have to repeat this?
PHYLLIS: They're hoarding the feeds.
JOE: It kills and keeps killing the feed.
FREDDIE MAYFIELD: Check this out, it reflects sideways but not up and down. Why?
THE QUEEN: Break it up and bring it down.
YOUR HIGHNESS: Are they sleeping?

PHYLLIS: What does it say?
FREDDIE MAYFIELD: We're not sleeping, we're dead.
OSCAR: She has a cold.
THE QUEEN: What are they saying?
YOUR HIGHNESS: She doesn't have a cold, she's pregnant.
MRS PEABODY: She has a cold.
YOUR HIGHNESS: I told her not to sleep in those satin sheets.
JOE: You bought them for her.
YOUR HIGHNESS: I did but I had no idea she'd really use them.
MRS PEABODY: You made the bed.
JOE: I did not.
YOUR HIGHNESS: And slept in it.
JOE: So did she and she slept in it.
YOUR HIGHNESS: And so did you.
MRS PEABODY: You made the bed.
YOUR HIGHNESS: And she slept in it.
FREDDIE MAYFIELD: And so did you.
YOUR HIGHNESS: I did but I had no idea.
MRS PEABODY: Yes you did.
JOE: You had an idea before you bought the sheets and that's why you bought the sheets.
OSCAR: And you got them half price.
YOUR HIGHNESS: If they hadn't been half price I wouldn't have bought them.
THE QUEEN: Bullyshit.
FREDDIE MAYFIELD: Ready or not?
PHYLLIS: Not ready.
THE QUEEN: This conversation, I can't go on with it.

YOUR HIGHNESS: Replace my voice with a voice over.
OSCAR: Which one?
THE QUEEN: B23.
PHYLLIS: All right.
YOUR HIGHNESS: Turn around.
THE QUEEN: No thank you, I don't want to look at you.
YOUR HIGHNESS: I want to look at you.
THE QUEEN: What?
YOUR HIGHNESS: You heard what I said.
THE QUEEN: You didn't say it.
YOUR HIGHNESS: Yes I did.
FREDDIE MAYFIELD: We've determined that this is not your own voice but an imitation of it.
MRS PEABODY: I want my money for the sheets back. I lent you that money and now you've bought the sheets and induced this pregnancy and I want my money back.
YOUR HIGHNESS: Who said that?
THE QUEEN: Get me my ashtray, I'm not finished yet.
YOUR HIGHNESS: Ashtray!
OSCAR: Turn the beat around.
JOE: Shut it off.
PHYLLIS: Shut who off?
THE QUEEN: Shut me off.
MRS PEABODY: It's me, Mrs. Peabody.
FREDDIE MAYFIELD: Turn it around.
OSCAR: Not my voice, not me!
JOE: Would you like some coffee?
YOUR HIGHNESS: I heard that.
THE QUEEN: I hope so.
MRS PEABODY: Shall we merge this?
PHYLLIS: I can't connect it to anything.

FREDDIE MAYFIELD: I'm not getting a reading.
YOUR HIGHNESS: Where are they?
THE QUEEN: Right in front of you.
YOUR HIGHNESS: You said you loved me.
MRS PEABODY: Who said that?
FREDDIE MAYFIELD: We've crossed currents and picked up something.
YOUR HIGHNESS: I changed my mind.
MRS PEABODY: Operator?
OSCAR: Coordinator.
FREDDIE MAYFIELD: Where is the feedback coordinator?
PHYLLIS: Who is this?
YOUR HIGHNESS: Cage fright.
THE QUEEN: Turn out the lights.
JOE: What for?
MRS PEABODY: Turn them out and shut up!
THE QUEEN: Put your clothes on, this is hideous.
YOUR HIGHNESS: From one who has returned thence naked.
THE QUEEN: Give me my shoe.
JOE: This is such a surprise.

• BENEFACTOR SPEECH INVOCATION

JOE: Oh, my benefactor and my something or other, I humbly prostrate in spirit before your divine majesty, I adore your sovereign justice and your infinite mercy. I am penetrated with fear at the consideration of your awful judgments, and my great ingratitude for your benefits, since I was ranked by invocation among your children, raised to the glorious dignity of an advisor, and thus entitled to enjoy you eternally in this office.

PHYLLIS: I was not then sensible of the precious grace bestowed upon me nor of the awful obligations I contracted when I promised to renounce the devil, the world, the flesh, the word. But I am now fully sensible of both and all three or four. I most humbly thank you for having brought me safely to the waters of your presence and I detest from the bottom of my heart every thought, word and action of my life which has been unworthy of advisor compartment officiate.

MRS PEABODY: You know oh your highness how often I have stained the robe of innocence with which I was then clothed, and how frequently I have violated my sacred promises, but you see the contrition of my heart and the sincerity with which I now renew in the presence of heaven and earth my profession of faith in the doctrines proposed to my belief by the directoire as well as the promises made for me when I was regenerated in the waters of this office.

FREDDIE MAYFIELD: I renounce the world with its pomps, vanities and false maxims which I despise because they are accursed by you. I renounce the flesh with all its temptations and sincerely resolve to endeavor to amend my faults, to conquer my passions, to curb my tongue and to sacrifice all that is most dear to me rather than again deliberately sully the robe which I promise to carry unstained before the judgment seat of the direct compartment.

OSCAR: Oh, your highness who did love me before I could love you when I was unable to implore that favor because of my mind and private concerns, look on me with compassion and grant me all those graces which will enable me to keep my engagements without reproof and loyalty to you. Agony and passion, torment, graciously hear me. All of my dreams are a heartbeat away. [*Last sentence repeated in Spanish*].

THE QUEEN: Thank you dear, now get up.

YOUR HIGHNESS: Get up I said!

MRS PEABODY: What is the decision?

PHYLLIS: Unanimous.

THE QUEEN: We accept.

YOUR HIGHNESS: Thank you.

FREDDIE MAYFIELD: Now what?

THE QUEEN: Now get to work.

OSCAR: Take him to his desk.

JOE: I beg that it may be received as homage since it is the most one could bring who returned thence naked.

THE QUEEN: Yes thank you, and put on your clothes.

YOUR HIGHNESS: What became of the others who went with you?

OSCAR: Dead, all dead.

FREDDIE MAYFIELD: What is the communique?

PHYLLIS: Diasporated, olvidated.

JOE: Would you like some pastries?

THE QUEEN: No I would not like some pastries, I told you I didn't want any pastries!

YOUR HIGHNESS: Empty that ashtray!

THE QUEEN: You're trying to turn me into a blimp. I don't want it in any vicinity of your memory motor memory!

YOUR HIGHNESS: No finesse, no delicatesse, you're mongrelized, violated, filth, intimidated, permanently suspended, excommunicated. Out of my sight!

MRS PEABODY: We're trying to convene.

YOUR HIGHNESS: Oh shut up all of you!

THE QUEEN: Phonies, balonies, balloonists!

MRS PEABODY: Careful of the warning signs.

PHYLLIS: I don't see any warning signs.

- **RUST AFTER CHAINS**

LAGRIMAS: And I quote, we have come here to your control room, your central casting, to the dome of your control tomb in your capital city, the very asshole of the universe to await your approval.

THE QUEEN: That's it? That's all?

LAGRIMAS: That's all there is and that's all there is.

YOUR HIGHNESS: And how would you know all this?

THE QUEEN: From my intimate knowledge of things, of evil and ingratitude, of black burned flowers, of funerals and burned toast, firestorms and disease and true ugliness and ruby red tears. Translation please.

LAGRIMAS: From my intimate knowledge of beauty and loveliness of flowers and tears of joy and gratitude.

YOUR HIGHNESS: Then my world is your world and your world is my world.

THE QUEEN: And my world is your world is mine.

LAGRIMAS: And we quite agree, don't you agree?

THE QUEEN: Completely.

YOUR HIGHNESS: Then what are you crying about?

LAGRIMAS: I just feel that something is wrong.

THE QUEEN: I wrote to you nearly every day, why haven't you answered?

LAGRIMAS: The notes have been intercepted.

YOUR HIGHNESS: I don't believe it.

LAGRIMAS: You have pacified my gall, take the torch and don't burn yourself.

THE QUEEN: Oh honey I'm already fried.

LAGRIMAS: I've been in this frying pan so long I'm burned to a crisp.

YOUR HIGHNESS: Does it smell much in there in your metal box?

LAGRIMAS: Not much, it smells like rotting water.

YOUR HIGHNESS: But our trialogue?

LAGRIMAS: I'm sorry but I've got to cut you off. There's an interruption.

THE QUEEN: Then it's possible.

LAGRIMAS: The humidity, the salinity will cause the molecules to disinte.....

Cut.
Interruption.

- **SECESSION ARRANGEMENTS-TEETH**

YOUR HIGHNESS: Cancel the secession arrangements.
PHYLLIS: We have to draw the line somewhere.
OSCAR: With a meathook if necessary.
THE QUEEN: Accept it, contravene it if you have to but intercept it.
FREDDIE MAYFIELD: We're getting something.
OSCAR: I have a new world for you.
JOE: It's an offer.
OSCAR: An invisible empire. I'm offering you a new world, an invisible empire.
THE QUEEN: My heart bleeds but I cannot accept.
YOUR HIGHNESS: All right then, it will be a bite to the finish and I have very sharp teeth.
THE QUEEN: I'll think about that bite.
YOUR HIGHNESS: And now I'm pooping mad!
MRS PEABODY: Don't say anything, talk is trouble.
JOE: Now, dear one.
PHYLLIS: What's the humming?
FREDDIE MAYFIELD: I don't hear anything.
THE QUEEN: Enough of your elephantine prognostications.
YOUR HIGHNESS: I'm offering you something.
THE QUEEN: Do you like to dance?
YOUR HIGHNESS: No.
FREDDIE MAYFIELD: Where have you come from?
JOE: I don't know.
OSCAR: Let her answer!
MRS PEABODY: Call off your goon squad.

YOUR HIGHNESS: They aren't a goon squad, they're very nice people with wonderful intentions and silvery tongues.

THE QUEEN: I can hear them sharpening them at night.

PHYLLIS: I don't.

FREDDIE MAYFIELD: Don't you hear that scraping at night? They're sharpening. Every night they get sharper but when are they going to use them?

OSCAR: They must be so sharp by now.

THE QUEEN: I'd hate to get cut.

YOUR HIGHNESS: We are not sharpening anything, we're rubbing our wings together.

THE QUEEN: Where is my engagement book, my schedule?

PHYLLIS: What city are we in?

YOUR HIGHNESS: The asshole of the universe!

JOE: Halt your clapper!

YOUR HIGHNESS: We only want to constrain them slightly, and now they say we have knives.

THE QUEEN: You are such a sad sack.

YOUR HIGHNESS: Who can resist the lure of Hiroshima?

MRS PEABODY: Will you be going to the cemetery celebration?

PHYLLIS: We have a communication.

YOUR HIGHNESS: Translate.

OSCAR: [*Spanish*] You are the embodiment of all vanity. High and slashing, beware of the slashback, the knives.

PHYLLIS: [*English*]

THE QUEEN: You are the emollient of all high vanity and slashing.

MRS PEABODY: Incorrect, say it again and translate, see how it sounds...

FREDDIE MAYFIELD: Launch the slashback and see how they like that one.
OSCAR: How does it sound to you?
YOUR HIGHNESS: Fine.
JOE: It sounds a little strange to me.
THE QUEEN: Is the verb correct?
YOUR HIGHNESS: I don't know if I can make that celebration.
OSCAR: Shall we answer the vanity or the celebration communication?
JOE: There's been an awful accident at the celebration, lightning struck the steeple. The coordinator was killed by the choir collapse on the communicants.
PHYLLIS: He was one of the communicants?
FREDDIE MAYFIELD: He was never able to receive the sacrament after his excommunication from and
OSCAR: By the choir.
YOUR HIGHNESS: Crushed by 30,000 pounds of screaming choirboys. A death worse than fate.
THE QUEEN: Poor things.
MRS PEABODY: They should have had a DJ.
YOUR HIGHNESS: Terra infermata.
THE QUEEN: But here he comes now.
YOUR HIGHNESS: I thought you were killed by the choirboys.
MRS PEABODY: I thought you died with the communicants.
YOUR HIGHNESS: Pulled asunder by the steeplechase.
THE QUEEN: Get me my prayer rug, my nose plug.
MRS PEABODY: That is not him.
YOUR HIGHNESS: Let me see you more clearly.

MRS PEABODY: That is not him.
YOUR HIGHNESS: That is not him.
THE QUEEN: Let me see you more carefully.
JOE: Ok, but be careful and don't touch.
THE QUEEN: I wouldn't.
YOUR HIGHNESS: Closer.
PHYLLIS: Close enough.
THE QUEEN: Closer, stop.
YOUR HIGHNESS: What is this?
JOE: Doctor I don't know?
MRS PEABODY: I thought we were exploring a frog's leg, a piglet fawn.
FREDDIE MAYFIELD: Oh dear, this is not him.
THE QUEEN: But it is.
YOUR HIGHNESS: But he's dead. This is a plague of ghosts, disconnect.
PHYLLIS: No, I want to see closer.
JOE: No, not closer and don't touch.
MRS PEABODY: This is not him.
THE QUEEN: Closer.
OSCAR: We can't get any closer.
MRS PEABODY: Doctor, what is it?
YOUR HIGHNESS: This is not the frog's leg piglet fawn.
MRS PEABODY: This is not.
OSCAR: But it's not him either.
YOUR HIGHNESS: Then who is it?
PHYLLIS: I don't know.
THE QUEEN: What is it?
OSCAR: It's me. Don't you remember me? We spent several nights in hell together.
FREDDIE MAYFIELD: I don't remember you at all and I remember every saffron face in that inferno.

THE QUEEN: That inferno, your saffron face, now I remember you.

OSCAR: The lure of Hiroshima. Who can resist it?

FREDDIE MAYFIELD: Get back from me.

YOUR HIGHNESS: Pull back, it's too weird.

FREDDIE MAYFIELD: Get that frog's leg away from me!

MRS PEABODY: It is not the frog's leg.

FREDDIE MAYFIELD: The dissection is a failure, change the slide.

THE QUEEN: I want a different view.

YOUR HIGHNESS: Weren't you at the birthday boat bash?

FREDDIE MAYFIELD: On the river?

PHYLLIS: Yes.

JOE: That's who you are.

THE QUEEN: What are you doing here?

PHYLLIS: Attending the convocation.

MRS PEABODY: Were you invited?

PHYLLIS: Yes.

FREDDIE MAYFIELD: Excuse me, there has been a rupture, a conflagration in the wires and waves and this is not him.

PHYLLIS: Don't you remember me? Some people were seen floating in the water. I was one of them.

THE QUEEN: I don't remember you.

YOUR HIGHNESS: Can you hear me?

THE QUEEN: Get him out, I can't look at his face for another sad, sour moment.

OSCAR: I was pulled ashore by the fisherman's dwarf.

THE QUEEN: I don't remember you. Get out of my palace you have not been invited. Who are the others?

FREDDIE MAYFIELD: One is an architect, 2 are translators.

PHYLLIS: 1 is the boss, 3 are intendants and one is a fool.
THE QUEEN: Thank you.
YOUR HIGHNESS: Thank you.
THE QUEEN: They were not invited.
JOE: I invited them.
MRS PEABODY: They are infiltrating.
THE QUEEN: Where are the potted herrings? I'm hungry.
MRS PEABODY: Don't bring those stinking things in here.
JOE: The cryptographer has been murdered bloodfresh.
YOUR HIGHNESS: Skip the murder for now.
OSCAR: You're sweating, you're angry.
YOUR HIGHNESS: It's all she can do to support herself and her baby monkey.
THE QUEEN: Cinderella. She's becoming distant, her voice is almost invisible.
PHYLLIS: Can't hear you.
FREDDIE MAYFIELD: He's a fucking bulldog, a bullfrog.
OSCAR: Don't provoke them.
YOUR HIGHNESS: Get the idiot board, this is all wrong. Let's cancel, call a recess and we'll start again tomorrow.
JOE: I'm sorry this has all been a mistake, can we speak again tomorrow? The queen is sweating, upset and tired.
PHYLLIS: Is she irritated?
MRS PEABODY: She's sweating.
THE QUEEN: You must excuse us we've just heard the news: our cathedral fell down. We are humiliated.
PHYLLIS: Excuse us.
YOUR HIGHNESS: But our response?
MRS PEABODY: We were hoping for a more flexible response.

PHYLLIS: But the cathedral...
YOUR HIGHNESS: How?
JOE: A thunderbolt.
PHYLLIS: A bomb the size of a peanut.
YOUR HIGHNESS: We're so sorry.
FREDDIE MAYFIELD: We've got to remove for a while and think.
OSCAR: About what?
THE QUEEN: About removing our wretched loved ones.
MRS PEABODY: In other words, we can neither confirm or deny.
YOUR HIGHNESS: Which means you do.
JOE: Yes, we confirm and deny.
PHYLLIS: Thank you, a more flexible response is not necessary.
THE QUEEN: Thank you for your patience and understanding.
YOUR HIGHNESS: We understand and remain patient.
OSCAR: To the point of provocation and irritations.
MRS PEABODY: Now thank you, we will meet again tomorrow.
YOUR HIGHNESS: I look forward to it.
JOE: And the lunch?
YOUR HIGHNESS: Festering in the refrigerator.
THE QUEEN: Thank you for your festering patience.
PHYLLIS: Not at all.
THE QUEEN: We're searching for the killers.
YOUR HIGHNESS: We hope they can be revealed and discovered.
FREDDIE MAYFIELD: Thank you for your good wishes.
OSCAR: Goodbye.

THE QUEEN: Bullyshit!

JOE: All I know is that was not the frog's leg we were investigationing at all.

YOUR HIGHNESS: And who was that man?

OSCAR: It was Lagrimas, our confidante, our codefendant.

THE QUEEN: Tomorrow there will be a proceeding powwow for the killings.

MRS PEABODY: But we're searching for the murderers.

YOUR HIGHNESS: And so are they and they think they've found them.

JOE: Where?

PHYLLIS: Here.

OSCAR: Us.

THE QUEEN: But we are not killers.

PHYLLIS: They've found us.

THE QUEEN: How could they find us? We're not what they're looking for. We are what they're looking for whether we're the killers or not.

OSCAR: And they have found us completely.

MRS PEABODY: But who is that man with the impediment?

OSCAR: Lagrimas, our friend.

YOUR HIGHNESS: He must be destroyed. Murdered bloodfresh. I want him in the morgue tomorrow mourning.

THE QUEEN: He has caused this hemorrhage of bad will and suspicion and get away from me! Your persistent, annoying image is shattering me!

YOUR HIGHNESS: Shattering me. You have shattered me!

THE QUEEN: My patience has festered long enough.

YOUR HIGHNESS: I've hatched an infinitesimal sparkling doubt about you.

THE QUEEN: What is this morgue love you have?

JOE: Who is that man?

OSCAR: He was using us to look at himself, I didn't want to look at it, he was using us to worship himself.

MRS PEABODY: Don't worry, things will automatically happen.

THE QUEEN: And all my beautiful boats were destroyed, my beautiful boats.

YOUR HIGHNESS: Forget about the boat bash.

THE QUEEN: Your mind is a malicious little pigsty. Prepare for the backslash!

JOE: I can't move myself to do it.

YOUR HIGHNESS: He must be reduced to the size of a crab's breath, a needle's eye, a spider's touch.

THE QUEEN: Goldfinger.

YOUR HIGHNESS: Exactly.

MRS PEABODY: You are reinstigating my despair and discouragement.

FREDDIE MAYFIELD: Everyone's got an axe to pick.

PHYLLIS: Don't pick mine up, you've got the gift.

FREDDIE MAYFIELD: What gift?

PHYLLIS: The gift of poison, you don't need a pickaxe, so put mine down.

THE QUEEN: Look at my face, look at it.

YOUR HIGHNESS: No.

THE QUEEN: Call in the cardinal, I want him to say a mass for Lagrimas. You may kiss me now.

JOE steps forward and kisses camera lens.

• 1. MR. MAYFIELD / HANDS

PHYLLIS: Hello, how are you Mr. Mayfield?

OSCAR: I've been thinking about your face in there. Would you consider leaving there if I was to make it possible?

FREDDIE MAYFIELD: The mice have eaten my hands, give me back my hands.

PHYLLIS: That won't be possible.

OSCAR: Such angry mice.

FREDDIE MAYFIELD: They're hungry too, they had to eat something.

PHYLLIS: But we share their famine you must believe us.

FREDDIE MAYFIELD: You don't look thin.

OSCAR: But Mr. Mayfield, my dear Mr. Mayfield, you're always thinking about eating.

FREDDIE MAYFIELD: My fingers are frozen, deteriorating, collapsing, disintegrating digit by finger, digit by digit, fingerprint by fingerprint and so on. They're leaping away from me flying, waving goodbye to me. I'm losing my fingers, gangrened in a gang off my hand. I'm losing my hands, what'll I do?

PHYLLIS: Just wait.

FREDDIE MAYFIELD: Wait for what? Till they all fall off to stumps? How will I wash my face or will that fall off too?

OSCAR: Have you touched your face with your fingers?

FREDDIE MAYFIELD: Yes I have.

PHYLLIS: What did it feel like when you touched it?

FREDDIE MAYFIELD: Fumbling in the dark as I felt my face, I could smell the jalapeño, the chili, the cilantro and the camphor combined. They've been poisoned with those gloves. Poisoned by my very own gloves to keep my own wicked hands cold, poisoned by my own hands.

OSCAR: Wrap your apron around your fingers.

THE QUEEN: No, he might think I'm a swan. I'm not Polly.

FREDDIE MAYFIELD: Really I'm not.

THE QUEEN: My face, my hands, what next?

JOE: Your beautiful torso.

PHYLLIS: Don't touch your face, it's too late.

FREDDIE MAYFIELD: She had to stay home, she has a cold.

OSCAR: Tell me why you're crying?

THE QUEEN: No.

FREDDIE MAYFIELD: There is nothing to tell, my hands are frozen to pieces.

THE QUEEN: Oh what shall I do?

PHYLLIS: I don't know, isn't it written somewhere in a book what to do?

OSCAR: [*Spanish*]

FREDDIE MAYFIELD: I told them to wait till tomorrow and then we would decide.

PHYLLIS: We've already decided. Tell them today.

MRS PEABODY: I think we should wait a day or so.

OSCAR: All right.

PHYLLIS: Any other message?

MRS PEABODY: Not a word.

FREDDIE MAYFIELD: My fingers are getting so cold.

PHYLLIS: Go get plowed.

THE QUEEN: That'll warm them up.

OSCAR: Get up off your knees and stop acting so beat up.

FREDDIE MAYFIELD: But my fingers, I can hardly feel them!

THE QUEEN: They're freezing up.

FREDDIE MAYFIELD: Be gone! Get out of here, you're no help.

PHYLLIS: Yes, your highness would you like a drink?

FREDDIE MAYFIELD: I didn't say I wanted a drink, I want to cut off my right hand.

PHYLLIS: Do you?

FREDDIE MAYFIELD: Get me that drink!

OSCAR: Yes, your highness.

FREDDIE MAYFIELD: Your serene highness!

PHYLLIS: Now tell me why you're crying.

FREDDIE MAYFIELD: My fingers. I'm worried about them they're so numb.

OSCAR: Is that better?

FREDDIE MAYFIELD: No, where is that ass's jawbone?

PHYLLIS: In the cabinet.

FREDDIE MAYFIELD: I will pick it up and when I get finished you'll all be finished.

OSCAR: Get her that drink.

THE QUEEN: I don't want a drink.

FREDDIE MAYFIELD: Then don't have a drink.

JOE: And stop moaning about those fingers. If you want I'll cut them off.

THE QUEEN: Where is that ass's jawbone?

YOUR HIGHNESS: But I also prayed that the young man who shot me would get well too.

PHYLLIS: Oh, how kind of you.

YOUR HIGHNESS: Oh, yeah.

OSCAR: How are we supposed to answer them when we don't even know what they're asking?

YOUR HIGHNESS: Anticipate.
FREDDIE MAYFIELD: But I have no idea.
YOUR HIGHNESS: You can't even make a guess?
PHYLLIS: No.
YOUR HIGHNESS: I rely on you to know.
FREDDIE MAYFIELD: But I don't and I'm so worried about my fingers.
JOE: Keep typing, I don't care about your animal agonies.

• BUDGET / CARDINAL / BULLET HOLE

JOE: Shall we start with the preliminary budget?
MRS PEABODY: First witness.
YOUR HIGHNESS: Cardinal Catinka.
FREDDIE MAYFIELD: Now, the bullet hole.
OSCAR: From the globo dextro a piece of lead weighing three eighths of an ounce was removed. And from the carefully executed autopsy and the attendant circumstances as established, it can be inferred with certainty that the deceased placed a loaded pistol in his mouth and shot himself with it.
MRS PEABODY: Death must have resulted very quickly from gunpowder asphyxia. On the strength of these indications and in the light of physiological principles, we are led to inform that the deceased was by temperament a sanguino cholericus in summo gradu and undoubtedly suffered severe attacks of hypochondria.
PHYLLIS: If it is true that this eccentric temperament was accompanied by religious extravagance, it may be inferred that the deceased was suffering from mental illness. And we know that's not true.
FREDDIE MAYFIELD: And what about her?
PHYLLIS: Her lovely blue coat was open and her white batiste dress revealed a small hole ringed with black and barely encrusted blood.
OSCAR: [*Spanish*]
THE QUEEN: We're not talking about the bullet hole.
YOUR HIGHNESS: We're talking about the budget.
MRS PEABODY: There is a hole in the budget.
OSCAR: Don't know anything about the budget.

YOUR HIGHNESS: You're here to give a speech, now give it and shut up!

MRS PEABODY: Can't you be more pleasant?

THE QUEEN: This is not a happy little land. There's nothing to be pleasant about here as long as you are under my roof. Now give the speech and shut up.

OSCAR: He wants to talk about the bullet hole.

YOUR HIGHNESS: Cardinal, no!

THE QUEEN: No one can deny that bullet hole.

PHYLLIS: The bullet hole is out of the question.

FREDDIE MAYFIELD: They're searching for the killers.

JOE: Isn't it true you are one?

YOUR HIGHNESS: Aided and abetted them.

PHYLLIS: They are the killers. They did it themselves, you have the killers and the killed in one gulp.

THE QUEEN: The budget.

OSCAR: I never gamble, it's against church law.

FREDDIE MAYFIELD: The budget.

OSCAR: Bullet hole.

THE QUEEN: Cardinal please and thank you and goodbye.

OSCAR: Ashes to ashes.

YOUR HIGHNESS: You're trying to use some kind of symbolism polluted by transparent undermeanings.

THE QUEEN: The hot hostility.

FREDDIE MAYFIELD: Precaution, he's a meat-eating carnivore.

YOUR HIGHNESS: I can hear those little angels singing, popping and crackling in hell.

MRS PEABODY: We're looking for the killers.

THE QUEEN: They were trying to undermine and interdict our union.

PHYLLIS: But madame...

THE QUEEN: Get me my painkillers.
YOUR HIGHNESS: The painkillers.
PHYLLIS: We are searching for the killers in secrecy.
OSCAR: There's been a secret murder.
FREDDIE MAYFIELD: Somewhere there's a killer in you.
THE QUEEN: Get out!
OSCAR: No.
MRS PEABODY: Get on your Pontiac and ride!
THE QUEEN: What is it about you that I hate so much?
YOUR HIGHNESS: It's uncontrollable, intolerable.
THE QUEEN: My pepperiness?
YOUR HIGHNESS: Not that.
THE QUEEN: Your drowsiness.
MRS PEABODY: Your highness?
YOUR HIGHNESS: No.
THE QUEEN: Do you think I'm made out of ginger bread? I will bury you.
PHYLLIS: Her uncontrollable assistant aide-de-camp.
JOE: Your highness.
YOUR HIGHNESS: Get on that Pontiac and ride by the light of the silvery moon!
FREDDIE MAYFIELD: They've trashed him.
OSCAR: The backslash.
MRS PEABODY: Yes, he's been hit.
OSCAR: What's the matter with her?
JOE: She has a cold.
YOUR HIGHNESS: She's pregnant.
THE QUEEN: What was that play I liked so much?
OSCAR: Calderon de la Barca?
THE QUEEN: No.
YOUR HIGHNESS: How are you?

THE QUEEN: I'm slightly high.
YOUR HIGHNESS: Drowsy?
THE QUEEN: No.
YOUR HIGHNESS: I want that musician silenced, not another note.
THE QUEEN: Is the rice cooked yet?
MRS PEABODY: Put up the dalkon shield, I feel an invasion.
YOUR HIGHNESS: The toll house cookies.
THE QUEEN: Shall we divide them?
YOUR HIGHNESS: Yes, and then give me one of yours.
THE QUEEN: Can't you see I'm saturated by his presentiments and promises.
YOUR HIGHNESS: It's nice there, isn't it. These things don't happen there or do they?
OSCAR: Where is the aide-de-camp Lagrimas?
FREDDIE MAYFIELD: He's been driven into a tundra trench as you ordered.
MRS PEABODY: Cut like a knife.
JOE: He won't live without you.
THE QUEEN: He is clandestine, reckless, provocative.
FREDDIE MAYFIELD: You have a cold.
YOUR HIGHNESS: Have we prepared the menu?
THE QUEEN: How are you?
YOUR HIGHNESS: What a smile, it's profound, violent, unraveling me.
JOE: Get ready for the abduction, the abdications, the seduction.
YOUR HIGHNESS: I'm well prepared.
FREDDIE MAYFIELD: I don't approve.
PHYLLIS: That doesn't matter.

YOUR HIGHNESS: How is the drowsiness?

THE QUEEN: Give me your hand. Vengeance is mine.

FREDDIE MAYFIELD: She's in a state of grace.

YOUR HIGHNESS: In which case I will personally blow your brains out.

FREDDIE MAYFIELD: Thank you so much.

MRS PEABODY: Cut hard and deep.

PHYLLIS: We've got a blowout.

JOE: That's bush league bullshit.

THE QUEEN: Where is my book of questions? You know I can't do anything without my book of questions.

YOUR HIGHNESS: If I don't have the questions I won't know what to ask or say.

OSCAR: Don't say anything.

THE QUEEN: If talk is trouble I want the last word.

MRS PEABODY: This cabinet is already ossified, filled with asparagus.

THE QUEEN: It will be torn apart. Limb from limb, tooth from jaw, finger from nail. There will be no more of this constant rawhide and tongue twisting in the torture cabinet.

YOUR HIGHNESS: What is this inscription? It's a cobweb, a gridlock, a concoction, a mudslide! Who wrote this?

FREDDIE MAYFIELD: You did.

OSCAR: He's convulsing in the ministerium bathroom.

JOE: The asparagus.

YOUR HIGHNESS: Your mouth has turned into a fuming fleshpot of rebellion and sexual innuendo. You are banished. Trash that man, break his heart and send him to the dumpster. Humpty and Dumpty, get me my sabre and scalpel.

PHYLLIS: How are you feeling?

THE QUEEN: Slightly dazed, crazed again. On the warpath again. My pen is bleeding. Get me my tommyhawk and go home, we'll continue tomorrow with half a cabinet.

MRS PEABODY: We're in a metal box.

OSCAR: And I've got cage fright.

PHYLLIS: You are forbidden to say that.

THE QUEEN: Doctor.

OSCAR: Here is a gift.

MRS PEABODY: I have a new world for you, the gift of poison.

THE QUEEN: Give me my cigarettes.

YOUR HIGHNESS: Give me a light.

THE QUEEN: I'd like to get a scrapbook.

JOE: Would you like a little face cream, you're looking a bit old today?

YOUR HIGHNESS: Where have you been? I've been worried, waiting.

THE QUEEN: I wish you had better penmanship. I can't read this.

YOUR HIGHNESS: What is all that handwriting on the wall?

FREDDIE MAYFIELD: The children.

THE QUEEN: Get out.

• BABY TRANSLATION

LAGRIMAS: My work is extensive in that area and so you'll have to trust me. Can I help you with anything?

FREDDIE MAYFIELD: My translation was born but it was an incredible example of incredible deformed mongolianism to the ninth degree. And so you see it had to be let go, dismissed.

LAGRIMAS: What will we get from all of this?

FREDDIE MAYFIELD: My ears cut off. The idea has become a repellant acid flashback, in and of itself as was the child.

LAGRIMAS: Oh, how stupid you must be to have been so stupid and snailskinned, to reject your little baby.

FREDDIE MAYFIELD: It was brutally malformed, unwired. Do you understand?

LAGRIMAS: I understand only one thing.

FREDDIE MAYFIELD: What?

LAGRIMAS: That your little mongolian is gone.

FREDDIE MAYFIELD: It was gone before it arrived.

LAGRIMAS: So we'll put it out of our misery.

FREDDIE MAYFIELD: I seem to be confused.

LAGRIMAS: We're standing on the same floor, how could that be?

FREDDIE MAYFIELD: And so what?

LAGRIMAS: We're breathing the same air, we're under the same sky.

FREDDIE MAYFIELD: We are not under the same sky, you and I.

LAGRIMAS: How can you say that?

FREDDIE MAYFIELD: I can tell. Your shadows are much darker and deeper than mine and so are your eyes. Your eyes are so dark I think they're strange and I don't like them.

LAGRIMAS: Is that why you're confused, confined to this mystery of the mongolian?

FREDDIE MAYFIELD: No.

LAGRIMAS: Let me put you out of your mystery.

FREDDIE MAYFIELD: No, don't. I'd like to keep my mystery.

LAGRIMAS: I'm offering you a gift, a new world, the gift of poison.

FREDDIE MAYFIELD: Could you repeat that again?.

LAGRIMAS: Are we being recorded?

FREDDIE MAYFIELD: You know that.

LAGRIMAS: I know that.

FREDDIE MAYFIELD: Stop smiling at me.

LAGRIMAS: This coffee is so black.

FREDDIE MAYFIELD: How stupid you must have been.

LAGRIMAS: Give up and go to bed.

FREDDIE MAYFIELD: Has the doctor examined her?

LAGRIMAS: She's given up and gone to bed.

FREDDIE MAYFIELD: I'm giving up and going to bed.

LAGRIMAS: Who is the secret correspondent to your meditation?

FREDDIE MAYFIELD: What have you made me into?

LAGRIMAS: Nothing.

FREDDIE MAYFIELD: You have made me into something else, pygmalionized me to win a battle I never wanted to fight.

LAGRIMAS: I'm only Lagrimas, the nonparticipatory particle. The doctor is here.

FREDDIE MAYFIELD: Please give me the missing segment.
LAGRIMAS: What's in this coffee?
FREDDIE MAYFIELD: Nothing.
LAGRIMAS: It wouldn't be poison would it?
FREDDIE MAYFIELD: No.
LAGRIMAS: A certain kind of half poison to get my butt on the floor so that you can find something out.
FREDDIE MAYFIELD: We know everything you know.
LAGRIMAS: But I don't know everything you know.
FREDDIE MAYFIELD: Do you think so?
LAGRIMAS: I think you know things I don't know like what's in this coffee.
FREDDIE MAYFIELD: It's lemonade.
LAGRIMAS: So dark?
FREDDIE MAYFIELD: Red lemons.
LAGRIMAS: What do you want to find out?
FREDDIE MAYFIELD: Nothing, give up and go to bed.
LAGRIMAS: Mr. Mayfield, don't you remember me?
FREDDIE MAYFIELD: Yes. I don't remember you. Do you work for me?
LAGRIMAS: Yes. It's me Lagrimas, don't you remember me? I've worked for you for years. It's me. Don't you remember me?
FREDDIE MAYFIELD: Not at all. Where is my regie-assistant?
LAGRIMAS: In your office.
FREDDIE MAYFIELD: But she has her own office. What is she doing in mine?
LAGRIMAS: I don't know.
FREDDIE MAYFIELD: Please have her come here. What are you doing in my office?!

MRS PEABODY: Getting the reports.

FREDDIE MAYFIELD: What reports?

MRS PEABODY: The reports you asked for.

FREDDIE MAYFIELD: Tell me which ones I asked for.

MRS PEABODY: Reports 3436 and 29 technotronic negotiations and the absolutions.

FREDDIE MAYFIELD: Correct. You are absolved. Isn't this coffee too black?

MRS PEABODY: It's lemonade.

LAGRIMAS: I thought so.

FREDDIE MAYFIELD: I'd like a nice, cold, clear glass of lemonade.

MRS PEABODY: How are you?

FREDDIE MAYFIELD: Slightly dazed, overbaked.

LAGRIMAS: The sun is too strong, the bug has bitten.

MRS PEABODY: Give up and go to bed.

FREDDIE MAYFIELD: Please give that evidence to me, the reports and so on. The bug has bitten and please don't leave me by myself again, it's too lonely.

LAGRIMAS: But the doctor is here.

FREDDIE MAYFIELD: Is he here? I thought I asked him to leave. Ask him to leave. I don't want him here, send him out of the compound. He's compounding the confusion in here and so I want him to go out of here and not come back, he's snailskinned. How could you be so stupid? Oh, how stupid you must be to have been so stupid to betray me.

LAGRIMAS: I didn't.

FREDDIE MAYFIELD: How stupid you must have been.

LAGRIMAS: Have some lemonade.

FREDDIE MAYFIELD: No.

LAGRIMAS: Have it.

FREDDIE MAYFIELD: Please drink it, drink the whole pitcher in front of me.

LAGRIMAS: I'm disinclined. How could you have been so foolish and stupid?

FREDDIE MAYFIELD: You've become disinclined, misled, snailskinned, mongolian.

LAGRIMAS: How could you have been so stupid. It's me Lagrimas.

FREDDIE MAYFIELD: You're beyond the threshold I'm sorry to say. You are going to take my order or resign, please drink the lemonade and you will be absolved.

LAGRIMAS: It is my horror duty not to drink the lemonade. I am a noncombatant, a medic, I cannot drink it.

FREDDIE MAYFIELD: You refuse the absolution?

LAGRIMAS: I refuse the lemonade.

FREDDIE MAYFIELD: Please resign or confess.

LAGRIMAS: You've started a strange joke.

FREDDIE MAYFIELD: And now you have to finish it. Drink the lemonade.

LAGRIMAS: What do you want me to say?

FREDDIE MAYFIELD: I told you to run to me if you needed a shoulder and now you have me running to you. That is not the way it was supposed to be.

LAGRIMAS: You've taken advantage of my aching head.

FREDDIE MAYFIELD: Have some coffee.

LAGRIMAS: It's bitter.

FREDDIE MAYFIELD: A bitter bug has bitten and that's why you won't drink it. Am I right?

LAGRIMAS: I put my head on your shoulder and you tried to cut it off. Am I correct?

FREDDIE MAYFIELD: It is my horror duty to inform you that you have repelled yourself from my trust. Send him to the preacher and have him interrogated inside out, absolved, and throw him off the Tallahachie-Bridge.
LAGRIMAS: What is it you wanted to know from me?
YOUR HIGHNESS: Shall we put an end to this trialogue?
FREDDIE MAYFIELD: Have you done anything that might be wrong?
LAGRIMAS: No.
FREDDIE MAYFIELD: Then why can't you drink the lemonade?
LAGRIMAS: Is it poison?
FREDDIE MAYFIELD: No.
LAGRIMAS: Cut a finger off until he answers and continue to the toes etc.
OSCAR: He hasn't said a word.
LAGRIMAS: Is he crying?
OSCAR: No.
LAGRIMAS: How many ears does he have left?
OSCAR: Two.
LAGRIMAS: No, don't touch his ears, we need his ears. And you say he's not crying?
OSCAR: Not a teardrop.
LAGRIMAS: How sad.
OSCAR: [*Spanish*] Where do we go from here?
LAGRIMAS: To bed, goodnight.
OSCAR: What about the doctor?
LAGRIMAS: Let him go.
OSCAR: Let him go where?
LAGRIMAS: I don't know. Open the door and let him go where ever he goes.

OSCAR: Shall we follow?
LAGRIMAS: No, let him go.
OSCAR: Why?
LAGRIMAS: Go to bed. And I want the coffee strong and black tomorrow.

- **TRANSLATION**

LAGRIMAS: I wrote to you every day, didn't you get my letters?
YOUR HIGHNESS: Perhaps there was an interception.
LAGRIMAS: Almost every day. Where were you?
THE QUEEN: But all those letters, thousands. I'm afraid there's been an intersection, a criss cross of some sort.
LAGRIMAS: Perhaps the ministerium intercepted the writings.
YOUR HIGHNESS: But every letter?
LAGRIMAS: You don't believe me? I wrote every day.
THE QUEEN: The correspondence has been intercepted.
LAGRIMAS: But every word?
YOUR HIGHNESS: But I wrote to you very day.
LAGRIMAS: What's happened to your precious face?
THE QUEEN: I've aged.
LAGRIMAS: How are things over there?
YOUR HIGHNESS: I wrote to you every day.
LAGRIMAS: There's been an avalanche at the hacienda but otherwise all is well in the horror house.
THE QUEEN: How is the ministerium?
LAGRIMAS: He lives in an olfactory world, his messages are relentless.
YOUR HIGHNESS: How are the messengers?
LAGRIMAS: The messengers are a mess. That's all I can say for now.
THE QUEEN: But I wrote to you every day.
LAGRIMAS: How will I know it's you?
YOUR HIGHNESS: You won't.

lagrimas: How are things in the disco?

the queen: I'm up to my knees in a pail of my own vomit but it'll be all right.

lagrimas: But how will I know it's you?

your highness: Up to my knees I said.

lagrimas: But I how will I know you?

the queen: Did you look in his mouth?

your highness: All his teeth were rotten.

the queen: It worries me.

your highness: What did his tongue look like?

the queen: Didn't see it.

your highness: It worries me.

the queen: How will I know it's you?

your highness: Up to my knees I said.

the queen: But I how will I know it's you?

- **SECRET HARBOR**

Wall turns halfway.
YOUR HIGHNESS: And what is that stinking breeze I smell?!
MRS PEABODY: The remnants of the boats. All your little boats. Your navy is rotting in the harbor after the storm.
THE QUEEN: Couldn't they sink them to remove the stink? Do we have to inhale that beat up smell all day?
OSCAR: It gives me disgust.
JOE: It's the sun and the flies and the bodies cooking in their armor.
PHYLLIS: We have sunk the navy. In fact it sunk itself but the bodies have washed up.
YOUR HIGHNESS: Change the direction of the wind.
THE QUEEN: Push it backward. Get it out of here, do I have to sit here and smell my empire rotting?
FREDDIE MAYFIELD: The wind will stop and reverse when the sun goes down.
YOUR HIGHNESS: How could I have inherited this?
MRS PEABODY: I don't know.
JOE: You don't know? Is that all you can say? Of course you don't know. All you know is that you don't know. What else do you know?
YOUR HIGHNESS: Well, tell me something fragrant.
OSCAR: Even the air is rotting.
THE QUEEN: What does the feed say?
MRS PEABODY: Nothing, we're not getting any feed from anywhere.
THE QUEEN: Why not?

JOE: There is none. No transmission.
FREDDIE MAYFIELD: There's no transmissioner.
THE QUEEN: Where is that ass's jawbone?
MRS PEABODY: The aide-de-camp?
YOUR HIGHNESS: Shall we pray save us prayers?
OSCAR: He doesn't understand, he's too stupid.
YOUR HIGHNESS: Oh, lord, get me out of this for the sake of this supply of defects, heretics, schismatics, libertines, asthmatics, atheists.
THE QUEEN: Blasphemers, sorcerers, mohammedans, jews and idolaters.
FREDDIE MAYFIELD: And everyone else who's come to this stinking, unbloody sacrifice./
YOUR HIGHNESS: Oh orgiastic pelican of disaster, bleed us no more.
THE QUEEN: Perhaps we've been too impatient.
JOE: Inky, dinky parlez-vous.
THE QUEEN: I told you never to say such a thing!
YOUR HIGHNESS: Perhaps we've been too patient.
THE QUEEN: Perhaps we've been too impatient.
YOUR HIGHNESS: Shall we wait an interval.
JOE: No more intervals.
YOUR HIGHNESS: Translate please. Because of your thrashing arrogance you have gone far beyond yourself into something else. You've become someone else.
OSCAR: [*Spanish*]
THE QUEEN: What have they said?
MRS PEABODY: [*German*]
JOE: Because of your thrashing arrogance you have gone far beyond yourself. You've become someone else.
YOUR HIGHNESS: But where are they?

THE QUEEN: Send this. They've hidden themselves inside a strategic hamlet created by their message machine, their interpreter.

MRS PEABODY: [*German*]

OSCAR: [*Spanish*]

PHYLLIS: They've hidden themselves inside a strategic hamburger created by their message machine, their coordinator.

MRS PEABODY: There's been a false report.

OSCAR: There's been a false report.

YOUR HIGHNESS: It was inoperative and so we could not operate with it.

OSCAR: [*Spanish*]

MRS PEABODY: [*German*]

FREDDIE MAYFIELD: It was inoperative and so we could not operate with it.

THE QUEEN: Bullyshit.

PHYLLIS: What about her experts?

YOUR HIGHNESS: Her experts are nothing but a cabal coffeeclatch of incendiaries and horoscope readers.

OSCAR: [*Spanish*]

MRS PEABODY: [*German*] Whoremongers and trailblazers, hacking their way into unknown territories.

PHYLLIS: Whoremongers and trailblazers hacking their way into unknown territories.

THE QUEEN: But Mrs. Peabody...

YOUR HIGHNESS: She's trying to therapize us with some kind of weird linguistic retraining of our human nervous system.

PHYLLIS: She knows we're nervous.

OSCAR: We're not nervous.

PHYLLIS: But the rest of the message is unclear.

JOE: Not so clear, some kind of syntactics going on.

THE QUEEN: Oh my dear, not again I cannot bear it.

YOUR HIGHNESS: Call in the theoretician.

OSCAR: Number 27 to the front desk please. [*Spanish*]

MRS PEABODY: But they know we disagree.

THE QUEEN: And wholeheartedly. Whole hog, pigglywiggly.

FREDDIE MAYFIELD: And we have all agreed to do so in every reaction we make. We signify our agreement.

MRS PEABODY: And so must agree.

THE QUEEN: Oh, I don't understand this.

PHYLLIS: You're not supposed to.

THE QUEEN: But I want to.

JOE: You don't have to want to and why should you want to if you're not supposed to and you don't have to.

YOUR HIGHNESS: But I must.

JOE: Don't take it personal, you're just a functionary.

YOUR HIGHNESS: What are you waiting for? Call in the theoretician.

PHYLLIS: What is she gazing at?

THE QUEEN: I feel a dread coming by. There, a natty dread lock!

JOE: There's no dread in here.

THE QUEEN: Please don't touch me, please don't.

YOUR HIGHNESS: I couldn't bear it.

OSCAR: But why, I'm your doctor.

THE QUEEN: Please don't.

PHYLLIS: But I must listen to your palpitations to keep track of them.

THE QUEEN: Please don't.

YOUR HIGHNESS: Isn't there any other way to listen?

THE QUEEN: Can't you look at my veins? They're pulsing.

MRS PEABODY: No, that won't work.

YOUR HIGHNESS: And get out of that get-up, that costume.

JOE: Don't you like it?

PHYLLIS: No.

THE QUEEN: Remove it from your spindly body at once.

JOE: I will not become naked.

THE QUEEN: You will remove it at once. Take it off!

YOUR HIGHNESS: Or have it cleaned at least. It smells.

FREDDIE MAYFIELD: I told you. That is the armada remnant and the rats.

MRS PEABODY: I killed the last one myself.

YOUR HIGHNESS: How?

JOE: I stabbed it with a stick. It was rustling around in the garden. I stabbed it and it let out a gigantic, squealing chill and inhaled a tire screech, it was thrilling.

OSCAR: [*Spanish*]

THE QUEEN: Oh baby please don't talk about such things. It's not good for me.

YOUR HIGHNESS: I'm so sorry.

THE QUEEN: Please change the costume.

JOE: Yes.

THE QUEEN: Please don't touch me.

JOE: You don't want me to touch you and yet you ask me to remove my clothes in your presence. I don't understand your presentiments.

FREDDIE MAYFIELD: And then you begin to talk about rat killing and bloodletting and chilling, screeching, what is the meaning of this?

PHYLLIS: What can be the reason?

THE QUEEN: Armadillo. I'm dazed, confused, excuse me.

YOUR HIGHNESS: I can't stand the smell of the cooking armadillo.

OSCAR: It's the rotting army armada I told you. The smell is similar because of the same way it is cooked in its armor.

THE QUEEN: Can't you peel their armor off and let them rot in the free air?

JOE: 15,000 Men? Impossible, we don't have that many can openers. The thought is repulsive, inundating. How long will those stinking bubbles of stench keep rising from the bottom of the harbor?

FREDDIE MAYFIELD: They only want to be free.

PHYLLIS: Champagne anyone?

THE QUEEN: It doesn't matter, none of them could read or write or barely speak intelligibly.

MRS PEABODY: Then how did they function?

YOUR HIGHNESS: Hardly at all.

JOE: How could they fight?

FREDDIE MAYFIELD: They were trained but never got the chance, now they're bubbles in the tide, one armed bandits.

THE QUEEN: This battle has worn me down to cinders, dust particles.

OSCAR: Is it raining yet?

THE QUEEN: Cancel the dinner, I couldn't look at it much less eat it. It would remind me of my wonderful little army. I would feel like I was eating them, one by one.

MRS PEABODY: Shall we just have the pecans?

YOUR HIGHNESS: Yes, and I'll shell them myself.

JOE: Would you like a hammer?

THE QUEEN: No more folk songs please.

YOUR HIGHNESS: My knights in shining armor.

PHYLLIS: The kitchen, the cook, the pots, the pans, the food, everything down at the bottom, completely olvidated.

THE QUEEN: No, I will never olvidate them.

YOUR HIGHNESS: They were the flying wedge, the first wave, the front line, the mystery phalanx. Out flanked and inundated but never to be olvidated.

THE QUEEN: Serve the rice and milk.

JOE: I hate that shit!

YOUR HIGHNESS: And so, not surprisingly you will eat it!

OSCAR: That stench is lifting me higher than I've ever been lifted before.

FREDDIE MAYFIELD: It's quenching me.

PHYLLIS: You're nothing but a downhearted moondog.

YOUR HIGHNESS: You've been harboring something in the harbor haven't you?

OSCAR: What harbor?

YOUR HIGHNESS: The harbor, the secret harbor.

THE QUEEN: What secret harbor?

YOUR HIGHNESS: There is a secret harbor, isn't there?

OSCAR: No secret, no harbor.

YOUR HIGHNESS: Yes there is.

THE QUEEN: What have you been harboring?

OSCAR: There is no secret harbor.

YOUR HIGHNESS: The rest of the army where is it?

OSCAR: It's all at the bottom of the harbor, I told you.

YOUR HIGHNESS: Yes, you did tell me but the rest of it? It's not all there is it?

OSCAR: Yes it is.

THE QUEEN: It's in the secret harbor isn't it? The rest of the armada.

FREDDIE MAYFIELD: I told you they're all dead.

YOUR HIGHNESS: They're in the harbor, the secret harbor where you have been harboring them.

MRS PEABODY: They're all dead and there is no secret harbor.

THE QUEEN: Call in the theoretician, we are going to raise the titanic lie you have told me.

YOUR HIGHNESS: A rat's nest, that's what this is, isn't it? And where is the secret harbor with the secret remnants of the secret army you have not told me about?

OSCAR: Get the interpreter and interrogate!

PHYLLIS: Not again, there isn't any harbor but the one we can see from here with the foam on it.

THE QUEEN: Where is the secret army then?

FREDDIE MAYFIELD: Why would you say this?

OSCAR: Cabeza de Cabrito, where is he?

JOE: At the bottom of the harbor.

YOUR HIGHNESS: Where is his body?

MRS PEABODY: We can't find it but we have an eye witness.

THE QUEEN: Whose eye witnessed it?

OSCAR: Bring me the eye that saw it and if you can't find it, I want that lying eye pulled out.

YOUR HIGHNESS: Where is the secret harbor?

THE QUEEN: Where is the eye that saw Cabeza go down?

OSCAR: Whose eye saw it?

FREDDIE MAYFIELD: Can I get a witness?

JOE: Yes.

YOUR HIGHNESS: Can I get a witness?

THE QUEEN: Then bring me that eye.

OSCAR: Where did your eye see this from?

MRS PEABODY: From the balcony of battlement number three it's….

JOE: But where...

MRS PEABODY: It's recorded on videotape, you asshole, don't interrupt me!

JOE: Where is the tape of the sinking?

PHYLLIS: This did happen. Am I right? He did not go down, he's secretly hiding with the secret army in the secret harbor.

YOUR HIGHNESS: That no one has told me about.

MRS PEABODY: Near an island somewhere.

FREDDIE MAYFIELD: Am I correct?

OSCAR: Maybe.

FREDDIE MAYFIELD: Then correct me.

JOE: Don't touch my eye.

THE QUEEN: Who will touch it? There seems to be some kind of disruption, a rupture, a lesion.

PHYLLIS: It's as black as an olive. Can it see well?

JOE: Very well.

MRS PEABODY: Then what did you see? Did Cabeza go up or down or was he there at all?

YOUR HIGHNESS: What did you say about the secret harbor?

JOE: I didn't say that.

THE QUEEN: Yes you did.

FREDDIE MAYFIELD: Bring me that little goat.

PHYLLIS: You are not to go to the disco tonight.

FREDDIE MAYFIELD: Please!!!!!.

MRS PEABODY: There is no tape of Cabrito.

JOE: I'm dazed, confused, slightly crazed.

FREDDIE MAYFIELD: Perhaps it's the sunstroke you're imagining you will have if you don't tell me. Would you like to spend the afternoon busting rocks and eating grits?

OSCAR: I want the body of Cabrito and your eye in that order and then I want the identity of the secret harbor where you have been harboring a secret army.

YOUR HIGHNESS: My dead army but your living secret army.

THE QUEEN: What have you been harboring?

YOUR HIGHNESS: I've planted the seeds of the olive that will eat me alive. Am I right?

FREDDIE MAYFIELD: By letting them rot and fester separated from everything but comic books. I told you, all they can do is kill chickens and now they will.

THE QUEEN: You've sown the seeds of the olive that will eat me alive. Mutations and pickaninnies, an army of little flowers that will choke me, a living morgue, a monsterama.

MRS PEABODY: Yes, your futurelessness. Waiting in the harbor he's sent an avalanche to the hacienda.

JOE: Balderdash!

PHYLLIS: They're waiting in the harbor where malaria is king. The best and the brightest, the least and the darkest. You've been secretly harboring in a secret harbor teaching them boulderism and terrification!

FREDDIE MAYFIELD: A conglomeration of intravenous subterfuge. The bug has bitten, don't you agree, Mrs. Peabody?

MRS PEABODY: Yes indeed, you've taught them only one thing. One word. A word to end all words.

OSCAR: In the end was the word and the word is with me.

YOUR HIGHNESS: You've been absorbed, assimilated, rejected.

MRS PEABODY: And I contra-indicate that you have been infiltrated, infected and deformed and we vote to abolish ourselves.

PHYLLIS: And thereby you. As your council electrocutors we have spontaneously aborted.

JOE: As compartment coordinator, I reject this abortion and dissolve you to the mud flats, effective immediately!

MRS PEABODY: You have been electrocuted we told you, you are no longer compartment coordinator!

JOE: Then what am I?

YOUR HIGHNESS: A veteran of gangbangs and girlie shows, there will be no baseball tonight!

THE QUEEN: Serve the enchiladas, cold if need be but we have to eat.

FREDDIE MAYFIELD: Do not serve the enchiladas, serve the armadillo.

YOUR HIGHNESS: Call the jumbotron, the telemundo and contact the space cadets.

THE QUEEN: What does the feed say?

JOE: Inky-dinky parlez-vous.

PHYLLIS: Inky-dinky no parlez you.

JOE: Parlez I say!

FREDDIE MAYFIELD: No parlez espanol.

YOUR HIGHNESS: Where is the scribe?

FREDDIE MAYFIELD: Drowned in his own ink.

OSCAR: Look at the way he looks at her.

PHYLLIS: Isn't that the look of love?

THE QUEEN: We've reached an awkward impasse, my compartment has imploded.

YOUR HIGHNESS: What's happened?

THE QUEEN: An upstart with a luxurious battalion of whispering pixies behind him. No assembly required.

JOE: A bitter fruit, a sour grape, trying to butter me up and have me for dinner.

PHYLLIS: The report, it reveals that in no uncertain terms, in certain terms, a second guess is required. Her confidante is the son of a bootlegging, swashbuckling creole.

YOUR HIGHNESS: With what?

MRS PEABODY: With tidbits and unspoken threats.

PHYLLIS: He's dead dedicated.

YOUR HIGHNESS: With what?

THE QUEEN: His arm, his leg, his legacy.

JOE: You're such a nebbish!

THE QUEEN: At ease.

OSCAR: What's going on over there?

YOUR HIGHNESS: They're having a bee-in, a shit-in.

PHYLLIS: Please try and be discreet.

MRS PEABODY: Repeat.

OSCAR: The secret circle, the secret square, it reveals that you are nothing but a swashbuckling son of a bootlegging creole, an untouchable.

THE QUEEN: A sour grape, a loose cannon trying to butter me up by making me bite the bullet. A bitter sour grapefruit with a battalion of whispering pixies whining behind you. I can guarantee you in no uncertain terms, blacklung.

YOUR HIGHNESS: Isn't that the look of love?
MRS PEABODY: No, it is not.
THE QUEEN: Isn't that a cigarette burn on the sofa?
JOE: No one smokes here, you know that.
THE QUEEN: It's a burn. Pure shame based poison.
JOE: You've had too much sangria.
THE QUEEN: You haven't had enough.
PHYLLIS: Call article 6, particle 9.
MRS PEABODY: The question of the seraglio.
FREDDIE MAYFIELD: You are accused of burning objects.
OSCAR: What?
YOUR HIGHNESS: Where is she?
MRS PEABODY: Burning objects.
FREDDIE MAYFIELD: What kind of objects?
JOE: Forgive me father, I know what I have done, I know what I done. I done my destiny and become a national jackass in the process.
MRS PEABODY: In revealing yourself you have revealed nothing.
FREDDIE MAYFIELD: Dereliction of duty, misadventures in full army drag.
MRS PEABODY: Does it hurt here? Here? Here? Here? What about there?

   OSCAR stabs the table with a knife.

JOE: Ouch!
FREDDIE MAYFIELD: What did you do to deserve that?
MRS PEABODY: Would you like to be a hamburger?
FREDDIE MAYFIELD: Call a lockdown. She's asleep, buried alive in the blues.
JOE: Yes, a hamburger would be great on the grill, the barbecue pit.

THE QUEEN: It's not going well I'm afraid. I want to fire everyone, I don't trust anyone.

YOUR HIGHNESS: Something keeps getting stuck in my tooth. Perhaps a drop of poison. Perhaps I've been too patient in my suspicions of plans for my removal. You've trashed your dress!

THE QUEEN: Oh yes that.. I don't like it. Too restraining, confining. It's a straight jacket. I felt like a jackass in sheep's clothing.

PHYLLIS: [*To* YOUR HIGHNESS] Give me that paper! You're contrived, constipated, co-opted. I have discovered, located the black olive of poison concealed in your incindiaristic repulsion of me. You're controlled by silly men in bow ties, screaming pixies and pickaninnies and penguinis twisted into a gordian knot around your neck!

- **PENGUINI**

Wall turns diagonally.

THE QUEEN: Where is my pet penguin, I loved him so.

PHYLLIS: He has suicided himself in disgust and disgrace at being your little penguin. He hated you.

JOE: Isn't that the look of love?

THE QUEEN: Turn the other cheek while I slap you! But sunshine, lollipops and rainbows, everything that's wonderful is what I felt when we were together. Brighter than a lucky penny when he was near. The raindrops disappeared and I felt so fine just to know that he was mine. What do you think of that?

PHYLLIS: I'll look the other way.

FREDDIE MAYFIELD: Physician heal thyself.

YOUR HIGHNESS: What do you think of that?

OSCAR: How did he do it.

YOUR HIGHNESS: A cobblestone.

FREDDIE MAYFIELD: There's a fresh wind blowing, they're having a dark celebration to exert their influence.

THE QUEEN: I'm under the wrecking ball today, but it's all right, everything that stinks must sink, my little boats full of cloven hoved pig legs.

YOUR HIGHNESS: My affection has been dislocated, something so beautiful, so ugly that the sun is on the run.

FREDDIE MAYFIELD: Why let bad bread bake?

PHYLLIS: You're an open clam suffering from sunstroke.

YOUR HIGHNESS: I saw a woman standing in the dark

with her baby on fire, a fuel injected sting ray, was that you?

PHYLLIS: Yep.

YOUR HIGHNESS: The poor little thing, what did it ever do to anyone?

THE QUEEN: My poor penguin, how did he do it?

PHYLLIS: He electrocuted himself with an asp of electric wire. He's hanging from the grill grid. No mystery there, a small bang, snapped it all away.

THE QUEEN: Don't come running to me with disaster on your tongue. Please don't do it.

JOE: I don't want to get involved in all these private situations but I suppose I have to.

PHYLLIS: It will be such a pity to leave you behind on our trip through the battlefield. You're such a good fighter, and you're so beautiful when you cry.

FREDDIE MAYFIELD: My beautiful translation has exploded into a million pieces and I can't pick them up!

MRS PEABODY: Why? I don't know, they're everywhere and all I can do is cry!

FREDDIE MAYFIELD: I'm not interested in your animal agonies.

OSCAR: Try to pick them up one by one.

MRS PEABODY: But they're all lost everywhere, scattered, shattered pieces of glitter everywhere.

THE QUEEN: Last night I became so ill.

YOUR HIGHNESS: That penguin had its teeth on my throat.

JOE: Any news from the mainland?

THE QUEEN: Deliver the goods.

YOUR HIGHNESS: I was struck dumb, dumbstruck.

MRS PEABODY: Is he crying, the wolf king?
OSCAR: Crying wolf.
THE QUEEN: Is there any news from the mainland?
YOUR HIGHNESS: We are one step behind, snowblind.
PHYLLIS: I'm not interested in your animal agonies.
FREDDIE MAYFIELD: But my translation. They've diluted it within the framework of the process and now we are incompatible.
PHYLLIS: Shut up and go to sleep.
FREDDIE MAYFIELD: But Mrs. Peabody...

- **PAIL 1**

LAGRIMAS: [*Spanish*] How many times have I told you?
FREDDIE MAYFIELD: Get off your knees.
LAGRIMAS: My fingers are cold.
FREDDIE MAYFIELD: Where are you?
LAGRIMAS: Not far away in a wire somewhere.
FREDDIE MAYFIELD: I forgot where I put you. Where did I put you?
LAGRIMAS: On a back burner. I wrote to you every day.
FREDDIE MAYFIELD: I have the letters.
LAGRIMAS: By the way, there's a tamale in the refrigerator for you.
FREDDIE MAYFIELD: I never read them.
LAGRIMAS: Why not?
FREDDIE MAYFIELD: I was in a profound state of illiteracy and discontent. Angst and anxiety, you understand? Have you vomited much?
MRS PEABODY: For every letter there is a pail of vomit, 3728 letters.
FREDDIE MAYFIELD: Let the punishment eat the crime. He will eat those letters, each and every one, no more rice. I want him to eat every letter on every page. Every word, written in…what was it written in?
MRS PEABODY: Blood.
FREDDIE MAYFIELD: Ashes to ashes, blood into blood. Out of the body and in again and out once again in a pail again. And I want you to save every pail because when he's finished consuming his scribblings he can start on the pails. Then he can have another audience with me in my infinite mercy.

LAGRIMAS: And then what?

FREDDIE MAYFIELD: There won't be a what.

LAGRIMAS: Goodnight. I'm going to bed.

MRS PEABODY: How can you sleep after looking at that thing?

FREDDIE MAYFIELD: No big deal.

MRS PEABODY: No?

FREDDIE MAYFIELD: You're crude and sentimental, and I want a soft pillow tonight.

MRS PEABODY: I will not bear witness to a bloodbath.

THE QUEEN: And I want a soft pillow tonight. Get my bath ready, that ashtray is full, empty it. Get the funeraria ready in case I'm murdered in my bed.

FREDDIE MAYFIELD: Yes your highness.

- **EXPLANATION**

Wall turns halfway.

THE QUEEN: This edict is valid forevermore, now translate it and get it out of my sight.

JOE: There has been an unprecedented intervention, the edict has become impregnated with humidity.

YOUR HIGHNESS: Salted water.

FREDDIE MAYFIELD: The river has overrun its banks, the sugar wind has turned to molasses, your message has become hydrographic.

MRS PEABODY: An unforeseen air bubble has changed our configuration. The consortium has consorted with her consort and wrangled a plot to destabilize the what…what is that word?

PHYLLIS: We have tabled your request.

THE QUEEN: Thank you.

JOE: What is it?

OSCAR: It was nothing really, they've taken the consecration and strangled it into some sort of plot.

JOE: Someone has begun mistranslating and then tried to guide it back to the correct translation and get it back on course. But on the other hand she wore a glove. The other translator has been doing the same thing without her knowledge being that he's dealing with another language and the only common language they speak is English.

PHYLLIS: The directives have been misdirected, misinterpreted, misaligned, tainted, maligned, transubstantiated into a holy misalliance of malice, mistakes and malformation.

MRS PEABODY: We're punishing you for your, for what?
FREDDIE MAYFIELD: For your curdled and violent language, it's useless and decadent.
OSCAR: [*Spanish*]
PHYLLIS: What has she said?
OSCAR: Anyway, in the meantime one of the architects of this alliance has suspected this and let it continue, desperately trying to follow it by using one of the translators as a syphon to the other not knowing that he is doing the same misinterpretation.
YOUR HIGHNESS: He has then been misguiding the queen into a bag of slander. Then on the other hand there is the case of the unknown, seen and unseen advisor, who we suspect is the ghostwriter haunting this proceeding.
THE QUEEN: Where is he?
FREDDIE MAYFIELD: He himself is here in absentia, by proxy of his own image.
PHYLLIS: So he's not here.
JOE: Sort of.
YOUR HIGHNESS: The third and possibly fourth and fifth infinite number of other circuits belonging to this filthy band of gypsies and fleshpeddlers is probably standing right next to you.
THE QUEEN: What have you done?
MRS PEABODY: I haven't done anything.
OSCAR: Two ghost writers and a possible third.
THE QUEEN: Who has ghost written my script?
FREDDIE MAYFIELD: Possibly the same person, writing both the questions and answers.
THE QUEEN: But who is guiding him? He couldn't have done it himself.

MRS PEABODY: Are you reading this question from a premedicated script of your own or someone else's design?

YOUR HIGHNESS: I'm saying it myself directly brain to mouth to your ear.

THE QUEEN: I don't believe that.

YOUR HIGHNESS: What about your answer? Is it also premeditated and given to you earlier to respond to the communication crackup?

FREDDIE MAYFIELD: Have the wires been infected?

PHYLLIS: Are we being eaten up and used as energy for something else?

YOUR HIGHNESS: A sweet, quiet corrosion?

JOE: There's always something under and behind.

THE QUEEN: You're a victim of the very songs you sing and that's a fact.

YOUR HIGHNESS: Get me my gloves.

THE QUEEN: They might be poisoned.

YOUR HIGHNESS: With what?

THE QUEEN: Itching powder, chili pepper and cilantro.

YOUR HIGHNESS: Horrifying, what it could do to my beautiful skin. It could eat up my hands and then what would I do?

THE QUEEN: You don't need your hands.

YOUR HIGHNESS: I need my hands.

THE QUEEN: For what?

- **COUNTING HOUSE**

LAGRIMAS: [*Spanish*] I have a gift for you, a new world, your head is an invisible empire, the gift of poison.

YOUR HIGHNESS: Where is she?

LAGRIMAS: In the counting house, counting the clear black drops of horror with her metalurgist.

THE QUEEN: My wild irish rose.

YOUR HIGHNESS: I tripped and stumbled as I was trying to search it out and now you see I've injured myself.

LAGRIMAS: I beg to differ.

YOUR HIGHNESS: Please don't beg here, don't subterraneanize yourself in front of me.

LAGRIMAS: And I quote "but put your head on my shoulder, let me comfort you as I see the words tumbling from your putrid metal mouth, your Hitler head, those pewter teeth, your tin headed god, and jackass donkey skin and saccharine scarab wrists".

THE QUEEN: Oh, no love you're not alone.

LAGRIMAS: I beg to differ.

YOUR HIGHNESS: Let me help you with the pain.

LAGRIMAS: Give me your hand, but look at it. It's a monster mash.

THE QUEEN: Please don't touch me.

LAGRIMAS: I wrote you every day.

YOUR HIGHNESS: Why didn't you answer my letters?

LAGRIMAS: You little stinker, spit it out.

THE QUEEN: I never got them, where have you been?

LAGRIMAS: I served ten years in a federal pigpen, subfreezing temperatures blew the lid off it and I escaped.

YOUR HIGHNESS: Poor Lagrimas, didn't he call you back?
LAGRIMAS: No.
THE QUEEN: He is calling you back.
LAGRIMAS: He is, yes he said so.
YOUR HIGHNESS: You were listening?
LAGRIMAS: Yes.
THE QUEEN: You listen to all of this?
LAGRIMAS: I listen to all the conversations. I have to, for vulgar language, it's part of my job.
THE QUEEN: Leather heart, are you there?
LAGRIMAS: One moment please, can you hold?
YOUR HIGHNESS: Surely.
LAGRIMAS: Now lay the chains and blockade the harbor.
THE QUEEN: But it is blockaded, already with all those sunken boats.
LAGRIMAS: Your little army of brats.
YOUR HIGHNESS: Go home.
LAGRIMAS: The boats were confused, swimming in circles.
THE QUEEN: Is this the coordinator?
LAGRIMAS: Feedback.
YOUR HIGHNESS: The feedback coordinator, where is Lagrimas?
LAGRIMAS: Where is Lagrimas?
THE QUEEN: Rotting away in a pail somewhere.
YOUR HIGHNESS: Breathless, disgusted, forgotten, spilled into intravenous weeping, a heartbeat away from nothing at all, absolutely nothing at all, and so, so delicately wandering. Oh, I just don't feel so good.
YOUR HIGHNESS: Are your fingers shaking again?
LAGRIMAS: It's me Lagrimas, I'm here to help you.
THE QUEEN: But I don't want you to help me.

LAGRIMAS: Yes you do.

THE QUEEN: But I don't.

YOUR HIGHNESS: But I don't feel so well.

LAGRIMAS: Please don't tell me about your agonies. Just give me your hand and let me hold it. I have a gift for you, a new world. Your head is an invisible empire, the gift of poison.

YOUR HIGHNESS: Translate please, what is she saying?

LAGRIMAS: And I quote, your head is an invisible empire, please don't touch me, it hurts. [*Spanish*] I have a gift for you, a new world, your head is an invisible empire, the gift of poison.

- **GOLDEN MOAT-TRANSLATOR REVEALS**

Wall turns completely, reversing sides.

THE QUEEN: Please try and think of something.

YOUR HIGHNESS: Oh, but I can't. Our consortium has become mystically impregnated, humiliated.

THE QUEEN: Where is the ghostwriter?

JOE: Headhunting.

YOUR HIGHNESS: You're trying to destroy me, to poison me again.

THE QUEEN: How's the water?

JOE: Clear, cold, calculated as usual, would you like a drink?

YOUR HIGHNESS: Where is the ghostwriter?

JOE: Bolted to the floor having a nicotine fit, nailed to his own cross by his own hand.

THE QUEEN: How did you get him to do it?

JOE: I've had easier crimes.

YOUR HIGHNESS: Where is he now?

JOE: I let him explode in flurry of ambition and vanity, the way I used to, and before I knew it he was bolted.

YOUR HIGHNESS: Get the crystal ball.

THE QUEEN: Get back.

OSCAR: Mirror, mirror on the wall who's the ugliest of them all?

YOUR HIGHNESS: What are we doing today?

FREDDIE MAYFIELD: We are trying to build a monument of words so heavy to crush you with its tonnage. Aren't you impressed by its monumentality, its magnanimosity?

THE QUEEN: Find a private hangout to hang him from.

YOUR HIGHNESS: What have you heard?

OSCAR: [*Spanish*] A voice in the wilderness, a ball and chain.

JOE: What did he say?

FREDDIE MAYFIELD: A voice in the wilderness, a ball and chain.

THE QUEEN: What did he do today?

YOUR HIGHNESS: He sat there all day thinking about one thing and one thing only.

JOE: And what was that thing?

FREDDIE MAYFIELD: The fountain of impurities we've created in our feed. He was trying to purify them for himself to try and find some particle he could understand. But finding nothing he threw himself on the pyre and became part of the breeze.

YOUR HIGHNESS: Now we are in agreement again.

FREDDIE MAYFIELD: How did that happen?

OSCAR: [*Spanish*] I'm sorry but it won't be achievable.

FREDDIE MAYFIELD: I'm sorry but that won't be achievable.

THE QUEEN: You have requested.

OSCAR: And we have responded whole hog.

YOUR HIGHNESS: We have responded in kind.

JOE: Oh, he's all goo-gah over it.

FREDDIE MAYFIELD: He's near death.

YOUR HIGHNESS: A sickness unto death.

MRS PEABODY: Here is the message:

THE QUEEN: You are a nonparticipatory particle.

MRS PEABODY: Your pillow is a chopping block, your cabinet is, diasporated, dispersed, monkeys in the moonlight.

YOUR HIGHNESS: Who is them?

FREDDIE MAYFIELD: Them is the monkeys.

PHYLLIS: Monkeys in the moonlight where thousands pass from the dark to the light, from this to that and yes and no.

JOE: Take off your mask.

MRS PEABODY: [*German*] I'm not wearing a mask. I'm the mind in the middle of the mask.

FREDDIE MAYFIELD: [*English*]

OSCAR: [*Spanish*] You must participate in the horror this time.

FREDDIE MAYFIELD: [*English*]

YOUR HIGHNESS: You will, whether you will or not, whether you will or won't.

MRS PEABODY: [*German*] My head is the gem of the horror of the horror crown.

FREDDIE MAYFIELD: [*English*]

THE QUEEN: How brave of you to admit it.

OSCAR: [*Spanish*] You are the horror.

FREDDIE MAYFIELD: [*English*]

THE QUEEN: And if I am you are.

YOUR HIGHNESS: Your horror is the frame of my beauty.

OSCAR: [*Spanish*] You're my crown, you surround me and protect me. My head is the gem of the horror crown.

FREDDIE MAYFIELD: [*English*]

OSCAR: [*Spanish*] I've poured you forth through my mouth. I sensed a force going out of me and it was you. I released you to surround me and protect me with your horrible thoughts and I'm free from them. You are the serpent king of your own dominion but your dominion is only my frame, my crown, my bastion, my battlement. But the battlement isn't the treasure it protects or the population inside.

FREDDIE MAYFIELD: [*English*]

THE QUEEN: You must be ugly, so I can be beautiful.

YOUR HIGHNESS: Is that what it is? I had no idea I was part of such rampant crocodilism.

OSCAR: [*Spanish*] Yes, indeed. You begged me to let it be you now and forever and now it is you and you don't want it to be you but really I had no idea it would turn out this way.

JOE: Is this a private fight or can anyone join in?

THE QUEEN: It is my private fight and you may not join in.

YOUR HIGHNESS: You only stand and serve and lose your head if you have to.

JOE: To serve something I don't even know what it is? That I'll never see or be?

THE QUEEN: Sure, you're my frame, my golden moat.

JOE: No.

YOUR HIGHNESS: If I am ugly then you are the ugliness I represent. You translate, you interpret, so we must be connected in some way.

OSCAR: [*Spanish*] We're connected only by light, in some cases not the same light. By wires and a few lousy unhappy unsatisfied electrons.

FREDDIE MAYFIELD: [*English*]

OSCAR: [*Spanish*] I've let it be you and you aren't all I need to get by because there are others and others who'll serve before and after you. Infinitely replaceable and irreplaceable but for now the word is on you.

THE QUEEN: But I don't want the word.

OSCAR: [*Spanish*] You are the word and you will say it.

FREDDIE MAYFIELD: [*English*]

YOUR HIGHNESS: No.

OSCAR: [*Spanish*] Go down Moses.//
FREDDIE MAYFIELD: [*English*]//
OSCAR: Deliver the delivery.//
JOE: It's too heavy.//
OSCAR: It's a heartache I know.//
THE QUEEN: It's an evil wind that blows no good.//
YOUR HIGHNESS: Oh, how lonesome you must be.//
THE QUEEN: It's a shame you don't share your love with me.//
JOE: It's a heartache.//
YOUR HIGHNESS: It's a shame if you won't share some of your love with me.//
OSCAR: But isn't it such a sweet thing I've told you?//
FREDDIE MAYFIELD: No, it's not a good or sweet thing.//
JOE: How lonesome you must be.//
OSCAR: But will you deliver the message, the mess?//
YOUR HIGHNESS: Hasn't she always. [PHYLLIS *sings "Share Your Love With Me"*]//
THE QUEEN: Why do you say such weird things to me?//
OSCAR: [*Spanish*] Because I love you. I'm your resurrection and light, from me everything that you are comes and goes. Dark and light and this and that, left and right up and down over and under and sideways.//
FREDDIE MAYFIELD: [*English*]//
JOE: There is no sideways.//
YOUR HIGHNESS: Who's been scratching on the window pane?//
THE QUEEN: And now I've run out of fools to help me and now I'm asking you to help me.//
YOUR HIGHNESS: But I'm a fool, what would you want me for?

THE QUEEN: Some foolishness.
YOUR HIGHNESS: Then let it be me.
THE QUEEN: Let me be your fool.
JOE: Then you are a fool.
YOUR HIGHNESS: Then I am a fool and I know it.

• GYPSIES — PART 2

Wall turns diagonally.

YOUR HIGHNESS: That was such a bore.

THE QUEEN: When was this written?

OSCAR: Sections were written on the plane in this direction.

YOUR HIGHNESS: I see.

JOE: And several sections were written in situation in the other direction.

THE QUEEN: What situation?

YOUR HIGHNESS: I see. Someone take him to the goon squad and introduce him to the boogie man.

THE QUEEN: And give me that report.

FREDDIE MAYFIELD: I haven't had time to read it.

YOUR HIGHNESS: I have, it is vicious slander and howling operatic outrage. Bury him with it.

OSCAR: But he's come all the way from the indochimney or somewhere.

JOE: Deliver the message that their representative of hooliganism and shenaneganism is not safe in our house. I don't like the way that tastes in my mouth.

MRS PEABODY: [*German*]

PHYLLIS: Who said that? What was that carnivorous grunt?

OSCAR: [*Spanish*]

THE QUEEN: Who are you, what is your name? Do you recognize me?

MRS PEABODY: Who's that?

OSCAR: He runs the joint.

JOE: Let me give my report.
PHYLLIS: Your bulwark is busted, you've been sunk.
FREDDIE MAYFIELD: But we were eating prairie grass in vast territories.
THE QUEEN: Whose territories?
JOE: Your territories I found for you.
THE QUEEN: For me?
YOUR HIGHNESS: Who said I wanted territories?
OSCAR: I thought you did.
THE QUEEN: Did I tell you that?
JOE: And your donkey skinned children, how are they?
THE QUEEN: Buried in an avalanche. Up to their knees in ice cream and mechanical dummy dolls, reeling and rocking.
MRS PEABODY: You've been sunk, out to the garden gadfly.
THE QUEEN: And our hideous little war, all my little boats were ruined.
MRS PEABODY: By you no doubt.
FREDDIE MAYFIELD: It was a hurricane.
YOUR HIGHNESS: Howling outrage, I said who is this man?
THE QUEEN: Who is this ridiculous little flip flop?
PHYLLIS: The physician who survived the expedition.
MRS PEABODY: Expedition to where?
JOE: To the territories.
FREDDIE MAYFIELD: He's the physician, mortician.
PHYLLIS: I don't recognize him.
MRS PEABODY: He's prematurely aged.
THE QUEEN: Stop handing me those bits of paper.
JOE: They're little thoughts I have for you.

THE QUEEN: I don't want them.

MRS PEABODY: [*German*]

YOUR HIGHNESS: Well don't give me any little notes either.

OSCAR: Do you know me?

THE QUEEN: Give me my shoe.

MRS PEABODY: What is your name?

FREDDIE MAYFIELD: What is your name?

PHYLLIS: Do you know me?

MRS PEABODY: Yes.

PHYLLIS: Yes.

FREDDIE MAYFIELD: Yes.

THE QUEEN: Animal mineral or plant?

YOUR HIGHNESS: Animal.

JOE: Plant.

YOUR HIGHNESS: Animal!

THE QUEEN: Then primate to primate. Who are you?

OSCAR: Who are you?

YOUR HIGHNESS: I thought I had gone to bed. Get out of my bedroom, I must sleep.

THE QUEEN: I will not be interrupted.

YOUR HIGHNESS: I'm not even safe in my own house, I cannot bear these interruptions, I need my sleep. I have to think.

MRS PEABODY: We are trying to convene.

THE QUEEN: Why do we have to do it now? Shut off the feed.

PHYLLIS: We are trying to convene.

FREDDIE MAYFIELD: Who is that?

THE QUEEN: Get that pamphleteer and mortician out of here, all of you.

OSCAR: I have a gift for you.

YOUR HIGHNESS: I told you I don't want that silly report.

FREDDIE MAYFIELD: I have a gift for you, the gift of poison, a new world for you.

YOUR HIGHNESS: What makes you think I'd want it?

THE QUEEN: You have strange dark eyes, what's the matter with you?

JOE: I've prematurely aged.

MRS PEABODY: Well, I have some miscellaneous notes.

YOUR HIGHNESS: Well, they're way over due. I do wish you had better handwriting.

MRS PEABODY: These are not miscellaneous notes, these are secret agreements.

YOUR HIGHNESS: And if they're secret, what are you doing with them? Now they're not secret anymore. They were for my eyes only.

PHYLLIS: Call the jumbotron, the telemundo. This has all been malcreated, clear the decks.

OSCAR: Erase everything. Trash it, it's all got to be re-entered, it's not a secret anymore.

YOUR HIGHNESS: And now that it's not a secret I'll have to change all my plans.

MRS PEABODY: You never had any plans and you know it.

OSCAR: [*Spanish*]

THE QUEEN: Get my scrapbook, I do wish I had a scrapbook.

OSCAR: Here is a gift. I have a new world for you the gift of poison.

THE QUEEN: I told you I don't like pastries.

YOUR HIGHNESS: Did you send them the poisoned pastries?
PHYLLIS: They are not poison.
THE QUEEN: You are all going to hell for this.
YOUR HIGHNESS: And forget all of these notes.
FREDDIE MAYFIELD: I don't want them anywhere in the vicinity of your memory box.
OSCAR: Diasporate them.
JOE: I'll never kiss those sweet lips again.
THE QUEEN: Now I've got a cold.
YOUR HIGHNESS: Now I'm going to sleep and if I hear another noise I shall personally blow the brains out of your already empty skulls.
JOE: But the pastries.
YOUR HIGHNESS: I'll have them for breakfast tomorrow, all right!?
THE QUEEN: That is an order.
OSCAR: [*Spanish*]
YOUR HIGHNESS: Just secretly listen to the feed.
THE QUEEN: He has no idea what's going on.
FREDDIE MAYFIELD: But I don't want my ears cut off.
YOUR HIGHNESS: Into the pantry all of you for the night. And not a peep, I must sleep!
MRS PEABODY: Yes your highness.
THE QUEEN: Serene highness!
YOUR HIGHNESS: Goodnight.
FREDDIE MAYFIELD: That's right.
JOE: Let's have a party.
OSCAR: In the pantry.
FREDDIE MAYFIELD: With the pastries and the pain killers.

PHYLLIS: That'll be fun.

MRS PEABODY: Don't we have to be at work early tomorrow?

OSCAR: So what!

Cut.

Wall spins ten times and stops halfway, splitting the stage front to rear.

• PILLOW TALK

THE QUEEN: Any words from the mainland?

YOUR HIGHNESS: They're snowblind, one step behind, kow-towing in some raunchy border town.

THE QUEEN: What are they doing?

YOUR HIGHNESS: They keep going inside a room and getting each other upset and hysterical.

THE QUEEN: What's the report?

YOUR HIGHNESS: Some strange dark numbers.

THE QUEEN: Is there any way I can help you? Anything I can help you with?

YOUR HIGHNESS: No, I'm sorry, nothing you can do to help me.

THE QUEEN: But why not? There must be something.

YOUR HIGHNESS: There isn't anything.

THE QUEEN: But I must know something of some kind to help you.

YOUR HIGHNESS: These are dead days for me. I have to wait a while till they pass.

THE QUEEN: But I had wanted to help you through them.

YOUR HIGHNESS: It's better that I walk through them alone and wake up with a friendly pillow. At this point even my pillow's turned against me.

THE QUEEN: But I gave you that pillow.

YOUR HIGHNESS: It's a pillow made of nails. I have to wait a while for it to soften up.

THE QUEEN: How long will that take?

YOUR HIGHNESS: Months or years or maybe hours but I doubt it severely.

THE QUEEN: I have to rest a while on it.
YOUR HIGHNESS: Won't it hurt?
THE QUEEN: Oh, it'll hurt but I have to take it.
YOUR HIGHNESS: Throw the pillow out.
THE QUEEN: It's the only one I have.
YOUR HIGHNESS: Can't you get another one?
THE QUEEN: No.
YOUR HIGHNESS: Why?
THE QUEEN: Because this one has all the answers in it.
YOUR HIGHNESS: Why are you so superstitious?
THE QUEEN: I hate to leave you alone in your room with that pillow now that it's turned its back on you.
YOUR HIGHNESS: Oh, it'll turn around, it's done it before but never so severely.
THE QUEEN: What if it won't turn?
YOUR HIGHNESS: It has to turn.
THE QUEEN: The screen's gone black.
YOUR HIGHNESS: It'll lighten up again.
THE QUEEN: But it's so black. How is your head?
YOUR HIGHNESS: Stuffed, puffed.
THE QUEEN: Who killed that man?
YOUR HIGHNESS: The gardener?
THE QUEEN: We know that's not true.
YOUR HIGHNESS: Who vandalized that man? Who has sodomized his mind, burned down his brain forest, suffocated it?
THE QUEEN: The gardener.
YOUR HIGHNESS: We know that's not true.
THE QUEEN: Is there hope we'll find out?
YOUR HIGHNESS: No, the screen is black, it won't tell us much more.

THE QUEEN: Who's left from that grim expedition?

YOUR HIGHNESS: Just one, Lagrimas.

THE QUEEN: And can't he tell us?

YOUR HIGHNESS: You saw his report. It didn't say.

THE QUEEN: Get away from me.

YOUR HIGHNESS: But I'm trying to help you off our pillow.

THE QUEEN: You're that metal pillow.

YOUR HIGHNESS: Get out from under my head.

THE QUEEN: Why can't I spit you out of my mouth?

YOUR HIGHNESS: I'm trying to help you.

THE QUEEN: You've turned against me and I didn't even notice. When was it that you turned?

YOUR HIGHNESS: It wasn't at a certain moment. It was slowly, softly. It moved forward step by step.

THE QUEEN: But why?

YOUR HIGHNESS: I don't know. I didn't notice myself at first and then I found myself on the other side of you with only an urge to trample you and make it look like it was your own feet that trampled your tongue.

THE QUEEN: But why?

YOUR HIGHNESS: You frighten me.

THE QUEEN: What is there to be frightened of?

YOUR HIGHNESS: Your eyes were getting darker and darker and at one point I thought they would finish me, turn me under so I stepped aside. I thought I was just stepping aside, getting out of the way and I had no idea I'd stepped away and to another side and reserved myself.

THE QUEEN: How is it that you could have?

YOUR HIGHNESS: I found that our connection was diluted, incompatible.

THE QUEEN: You're stagnant, repulsive.

YOUR HIGHNESS: I may be but your eyes were so dark and biting.

THE QUEEN: How many times have you tried to poison me?

YOUR HIGHNESS: Once or twice.

THE QUEEN: But with what?

YOUR HIGHNESS: A book, a word, a thought. Those little scraps of paper, those little thoughts for you.

THE QUEEN: I never read those scraps.

YOUR HIGHNESS: Good for you.

THE QUEEN: Don't forget what you are.

YOUR HIGHNESS: What's that?

THE QUEEN: Just a head on an unfriendly iron pillow now.

YOUR HIGHNESS: Nothing else?

THE QUEEN: Shall we meet again?

YOUR HIGHNESS: No, I don't think so.

THE QUEEN: Perhaps I've been too impatient.

YOUR HIGHNESS: I don't think so.

THE QUEEN: Where are you going?

YOUR HIGHNESS: To the secret harbor to wait till your pillow overtakes you.

THE QUEEN: How long do you think it will take?

YOUR HIGHNESS: Not very long.

THE QUEEN: But be careful, that pillow is ruthless. It won't be satisfied with only my head. It howls at night longing to be satisfied.

YOUR HIGHNESS: I'll try to avoid it.

THE QUEEN: Please do. I'd hate for you to suffer the way I have. Do you believe me?

YOUR HIGHNESS: Yes.

THE QUEEN: It's a very hard pillow. I don't think it will soften up until it's satisfied and I really think it'll never satisfy itself until the head it rests on is satisfied and that will never happen.

YOUR HIGHNESS: What's the final point of satisfaction?

THE QUEEN: There isn't one and so the pillow will continue to consume, never expecting a stalemate.

YOUR HIGHNESS: But it's not the pillow.

THE QUEEN: It's the head on the pillow.

YOUR HIGHNESS: How did you find this out?

THE QUEEN: One morning I woke up in a triangle of sweat and there was no way out of it. I found that I could keep expanding it, second by second if I wanted to and so I did but as it expanded it shrank around my neck at the same time. It was uncontrollable in any direction. It went in all directions at the same time always with a smile on its face until it was too large and too small to see at one glance and that's when I knew the tender trap I had fallen into. And so this pillow will be yours. You can give it away to someone else but not until it's finished with you. But you'll be finished with it before it's finished with you.

YOUR HIGHNESS: How will I know?

THE QUEEN: Don't you know?

YOUR HIGHNESS: No.

THE QUEEN: Of course not. But your eyes are dark, triangular, perspiring faintly, fatally bloodshot. When you've had too much bloodwine.

YOUR HIGHNESS: I thought I was one step behind you.

THE QUEEN: No, we've finished together, side by side, a tie, a stalemate.

YOUR HIGHNESS: Together the way we wanted it to be.
THE QUEEN: Both inside the triangle.
YOUR HIGHNESS: So this is the night that will kill me.
THE QUEEN: Oh, holy night.
YOUR HIGHNESS: What about the pillow?
THE QUEEN: You're my pillow and I'm yours but we've satisfied each other. We can give the pillow away.
YOUR HIGHNESS: And us?
THE QUEEN: Cancelled, finally satisfied, no more howling.
YOUR HIGHNESS: Isn't that the look of love?
THE QUEEN: Can you see me?
YOUR HIGHNESS: No.
THE QUEEN: Then I don't think so.
YOUR HIGHNESS: Then what is it?
THE QUEEN: I suppose a sort of bilateral plundering to the point of satisfaction.
YOUR HIGHNESS: But I don't feel so satisfied.
THE QUEEN: No sunshine, lollipops and rainbows?
YOUR HIGHNESS: A small thunderstorm and a light rain.
THE QUEEN: Didn't you want to be together?
YOUR HIGHNESS: But not like this, buried together inside each other.
THE QUEEN: But please don't cry, you'll rust the pillow and stain us.
YOUR HIGHNESS: We've been olvidated, obliterated.
THE QUEEN: Yes indeed.
YOUR HIGHNESS: Goodnight.
THE QUEEN: Shall we close the file?
YOUR HIGHNESS: Closed.
THE QUEEN: See you in the morning.

YOUR HIGHNESS: But please don't cry you'll stain our pillow, it's so clean and we've got a long journey ahead of us.
THE QUEEN: Goodnight.

- **PAIL 2**

LAGRIMAS appears on video as an old woman.

LAGRIMAS: Hello.

YOUR HIGHNESS: Now, who is it?

LAGRIMAS: It's me, Lagrimas.

THE QUEEN: How long have you been in there?

LAGRIMAS: 25 years.

YOUR HIGHNESS: It took you that long to eat the letters and the corresponding pails?

LAGRIMAS: Yes.

OSCAR: How are you?

THE QUEEN: I didn't think you'd survive.

LAGRIMAS: Oh, they were quite nutritious.

YOUR HIGHNESS: You've aged.

LAGRIMAS: You've aged, your face has fallen into your lap.

THE QUEEN: Give him a steak tonight, filet mignon raw.

YOUR HIGHNESS: And every night until a landslide comes out of every pore and then to the graveyard dead or alive whichever comes first. Has he written any more letters?

LAGRIMAS: Yes.

THE QUEEN: What is he writing them with?

LAGRIMAS: Fingernail and bloodrust.

YOUR HIGHNESS: Where are they?

LAGRIMAS: They weren't addressed to you.

THE QUEEN: Why not?

PHYLLIS: They were addressed to himself, it's a secret correspondence.

YOUR HIGHNESS: Open all the letters and tell me what's in them.

OSCAR: We have.

THE QUEEN: Without my permission and orders?

YOUR HIGHNESS: Trade places with the man in the box, you aren't looking too well.

OSCAR: Yeah, fuck you!

LAGRIMAS: Please take off that apron.

THE QUEEN: No.

LAGRIMAS: Please.

YOUR HIGHNESS: Tell me why.

LAGRIMAS: I shall tell of a hunter whose life was undone by the cruel hand of evil at the setting of the sun. His arrow was loosed and it flew through the dark and his true love was slain as the shaft found its mark. She'd her apron wrapped about her and he took her for a swan. And it's so, and alas it was she, Polly Von.

He ran up beside her and found it was she. He turned away his head for he could not bear to see. He lifted her up and found she was dead. A fountain of tears for his true love he shed. He bore her away to his home by the sea crying, "father, oh father I've murdered poor Polly. I've killed my fair love in the flower of her life. I always intended that she'd be my wife. She'd her apron wrapped about her and I took her for a swan. And it's so and alas it was she, Polly Von." He roamed near the place where his true love was slain. He wept bitter tears but his cries were all in vain. So please take off that apron.

YOUR HIGHNESS: So what. A silly story of pork bellyisms and schwein cottelet, I'm not Polly.

LAGRIMAS: Such a cruel and disgusting punishment, please take off the apron.

THE QUEEN: Section one of the peanut code, read it!

LAGRIMAS: The river is very wide here at this point as you can see. Nothing can stop me but disease and disintegration. But not for long, your expedition has resulted in disgust.

YOUR HIGHNESS: And what happened to that poor man?

LAGRIMAS: My lungs vomited smoke, a fountain of lead and gold, frankincense and myhrr.

YOUR HIGHNESS: This takes the cake.

LAGRIMAS: My compassion is bled by the prospect of your not taking that apron off. All my work is motivated by a need to die, you know that. My work is extensive in that area, you will have to trust me.

YOUR HIGHNESS: What a barbarity. Lagrimas, do you renounce satan and all his jerks and will you drink the lemonade?

LAGRIMAS: Goodnight Polly.

- **DOCTOR VISITS**

Wall turns diagonally.
YOUR HIGHNESS: Something is strange here. The bug has bitten, a painful and paralyzing bite.
THE QUEEN: Why do you keep examining?
YOUR HIGHNESS: Do you know you're diabetic?
THE QUEEN: No.
YOUR HIGHNESS: We must lay back for a while and then move forward with monstrous premeditation.
THE QUEEN: Lay back for a while.
YOUR HIGHNESS: A backslash.
THE QUEEN: Breathe in again.
YOUR HIGHNESS: What are you listening to?
THE QUEEN: Your heart, the sinspot.
YOUR HIGHNESS: Don't I have any privacy?
THE QUEEN: I have to listen to your heart to see if anything is wrong.
YOUR HIGHNESS: What do you hear?
THE QUEEN: Rock steady, I hear a phone ringing.
YOUR HIGHNESS: In my heart?
THE QUEEN: Yes.
YOUR HIGHNESS: Answer it.
THE QUEEN: Do you know you're diabetic?
YOUR HIGHNESS: You're lying to me. You aren't my doctor, you're an infiltration. You've always told me I was healthy. You have told the whole lie and nothing but a lie, the whole enchilada.
THE QUEEN: You're suffering, I must be truthful.

YOUR HIGHNESS: Do I look like I'm suffering?

THE QUEEN: You've had so many vicious interludes you must be suffering.

YOUR HIGHNESS: Wrong.

THE QUEEN: I'm suffering as much as you are, if not more.

YOUR HIGHNESS: Would you like to suffer as much as I do?

THE QUEEN: No.

YOUR HIGHNESS: I can arrange it.

THE QUEEN: I'll have you kidnapped and plunged to your death, how would you like that?

YOUR HIGHNESS: I must be truthful, give me that. What do you see?

THE QUEEN: Physician heal thyself.

YOUR HIGHNESS: I can see the veins in your hands. I can see through your skin, it's transparent.

THE QUEEN: Is that right?

YOUR HIGHNESS: I see right to the inside.

THE QUEEN: You're radiant, soulless. There's no inside. If there's no inside, there's no outside.

YOUR HIGHNESS: If there's no outside, there's nothing there at all.

THE QUEEN: Your invisibility has betrayed you.

YOUR HIGHNESS: What illness are you accusing me of?

THE QUEEN: Yes you are.

YOUR HIGHNESS: What do you see?

THE QUEEN: Nothing but dead.

YOUR HIGHNESS: Your death shines like the sun at the end of the day.

THE QUEEN: I give thanks to the one who brought it.

YOUR HIGHNESS: So these are the days that will kill me.
THE QUEEN: Yes, my dear that is the way it must be.
YOUR HIGHNESS: Thank you, goodnight and goodbye.
THE QUEEN: Have you contacted an angel at all about your leaving us?
YOUR HIGHNESS: Not yet.
THE QUEEN: Well, you should soon.
YOUR HIGHNESS: There don't seem to be many around.
THE QUEEN: Let's see if I can contact someone. An angel, a donkey, a magic man.
YOUR HIGHNESS: Who has bitten me, who bit me, what bit me?
THE QUEEN: I'd hate to leave this world alone, why don't you come along?
YOUR HIGHNESS: But I don't want to. Let me know if you change your mind.
PHYLLIS: Don't touch her she's in a sunshine state. She thinks she's an ashtray, she's hungry beyond the threshold.
JOE: And it is my horror duty to tell you that an avalanche of goodwill has crushed the hacienda.
THE QUEEN: Oh, my darling.
YOUR HIGHNESS: But how can that be? You are my garbage can, my ashtray, my ashcan.
JOE: Don't touch her.
THE QUEEN: How could this be? I put the ashtray on your face.
YOUR HIGHNESS: But I had such great expectations.
THE QUEEN: All that glitters is glitter and glitter only.
YOUR HIGHNESS: Somehow I must get through.
OSCAR: He's died of a violent cramp.

THE QUEEN: Where's my doll?

MRS PEABODY: You're shivering, quivering.

YOUR HIGHNESS: I'd like a few minutes alone with my corpse.

PHYLLIS: We can't leave you alone.

MRS PEABODY: There are noises coming out of him.

THE QUEEN: If somewhere among your little troubles you can help me with these little monsters.

FREDDIE MAYFIELD: What happened to you?

YOUR HIGHNESS: The gag order.

PHYLLIS: Whose?

THE QUEEN: My own.

JOE: Gagged by your own order.

YOUR HIGHNESS: Rather than betray myself. I've been gagged by my order in a jump in the order of command, the code of conduct, double crossed.

THE QUEEN: Rats deserting a stinking ship and oh I can't blame them, this ship was stinking, fermenting into something.

MRS PEABODY: Well it's fermented into what it is now. Stinking more than ever.

THE QUEEN: Nose plug please.

PHYLLIS: Do you smell it?

YOUR HIGHNESS: Please warn our friends.

THE QUEEN: The maharani and the pygmy tyrant, T-rex.

YOUR HIGHNESS: Bang the gong.

JOE: All right.

OSCAR: I'm sorry but this has all blossomed into a disaster.

PHYLLIS: I'm sorry for you.

MRS PEABODY: You are ugly, dirty and alone.

THE QUEEN: How are your sentiments?

FREDDIE MAYFIELD: An eyesore, severe, atomic, inflammatory.

JOE: Where are lord and lady asshole?

PHYLLIS: They strung them up.

FREDDIE MAYFIELD: They tried to avoid the killings and mutilations but they slew every column in the palace. Thirteen cities were destroyed.

MRS PEABODY: Whole counties were famished, so am I.

THE QUEEN: And so we will withdraw to our tiny island and hold on for dear life.

YOUR HIGHNESS: And what about my brain forest?

MRS PEABODY: Burned to the ground.

THE QUEEN: My brain forest full of humble, hunchbacked men with beautiful brains and soft, gentle sentiments.

JOE: It's been fumbled, bumbled.

OSCAR: They've corrupted each other and drowned in their own saliva.

YOUR HIGHNESS: And what about me?

FREDDIE MAYFIELD: The water will wash you away, termites will eat your wooden feet.

THE QUEEN: Out of the darkness and despair you have brought me a coal mine.

YOUR HIGHNESS: Abandon ship.

PHYLLIS: It's run amuck.

THE QUEEN: We have been rejected and our manifesto has been burned.

YOUR HIGHNESS: They sacked the city and took it away in a sack.

THE QUEEN: You are an evil thing. How can I be rid of you?

YOUR HIGHNESS: You said you could move mountains.

THE QUEEN: The mountain has come to Mohammed.

YOUR HIGHNESS: You are rid of me, don't you remember? You've suffered a massive blowout. You've been bagged, gagged.

THE QUEEN: Thank god and now you who started this cataclysmia.

YOUR HIGHNESS: You're such a sad sack.

THE QUEEN: There's a hostility loose in this room.

YOUR HIGHNESS: Leave it alone, it's looking for a friend.

THE QUEEN: Can't they operate to save me?

YOUR HIGHNESS: You're beyond safe.

THE QUEEN: But I've struggled through five centuries of rotten rebellion and egg in my face.

FREDDIE MAYFIELD: You've got the sting of Ishmael on your neck.

YOUR HIGHNESS: Oh, Miss Peabody.

MRS PEABODY: I'm sorry your highness, but we've unraveled. [*German*]

THE QUEEN: I'm sorry we've unraveled.

YOUR HIGHNESS: But I wrote you every day.

THE QUEEN: How could I have been so disinherited?

YOUR HIGHNESS: Is there a curtain around me?

THE QUEEN: Yes.

YOUR HIGHNESS: I thought so.

THE QUEEN: I told you some day I was going to kill you but I haven't figured out a way yet.

FREDDIE MAYFIELD: Too late.

THE QUEEN: You took me as your lover and forced me to betray my own people and cannibalize myself.

YOUR HIGHNESS: I'm taking you away in a cloud of our own blood.

THE QUEEN: But day by day, a death beyond belief, in time you will come to grief and then you'll be satisfied.
YOUR HIGHNESS: I don't even know how old I am anymore.
THE QUEEN: I'm leaving.
YOUR HIGHNESS: Don't go out you'll catch your death.
THE QUEEN: I wrote you every day.
YOUR HIGHNESS: The dog and the pig have been very good friends for thousands of years, so why stop a good thing?
THE QUEEN: Yes, we have.
YOUR HIGHNESS: But our consortium.
FREDDIE MAYFIELD: Gentlemen, start your engines.

- **ARRIVAL OF THE FILTHY BAND OF GYPSIES / CABEZA SPEECH**

Wall turns halfway.

THE QUEEN: Where are my pain killers?

YOUR HIGHNESS: They're not yours to take.

THE QUEEN: Here they come, his hideous little coterie.

YOUR HIGHNESS: The filthy band of gypsies, they've arrived.

FREDDIE MAYFIELD: Among all the princes who have reigned, I know of none who has enjoyed the universal esteem of your majesty at this day when strangers vie in approbation with those motivated by gin and loyalty. Although everyone wants what advantage may be gained from ambition and action we see everywhere great inequalities of fortune, brought about not by conduct but by accident and not though anybody's fault but as the will of god. Thus the deeds of one far exceed his expectation while another can show no higher proof of purpose than his fruitless effort, and even the effort may go unnoticed.

THE QUEEN: Oh, what a bore.

PHYLLIS: I can say for myself that I undertook the march abroad on royal authorization, with a firm trust that my service would be as evident and distinguished as my ancestors and that I would not need to speak to be counted among those your majesty honors for diligence and fidelity in affairs of state. But my council and constancy availed nothing toward those objectives we set out to gain in your interests for our sins. In fact no other of the many armed expeditions into those parts has found itself in such dire straits as ours or come to so futile and fatal a concussion.

OSCAR: My only remaining duty is to transmit what I saw and heard in the nine years I wandered lost and miserable over many remote lands. I hope in some measure to convey to your majesty not merely a report of positions and distances flora and fauna but of the customs of the numerous barbarous people I talked with and dwelt among, as well as any other matters I could hear of or observe.

MRS PEABODY: My hope of going out from among those nations was always small, nevertheless, I made a point of remembering all the particulars so that should god our lord eventually please to bring me where I am now, I might testify to my exertion in the royal behalf.

JOE: Since this narrative in my opinion, is of no trivial value for those who go in your name to subdue those countries and bring them to a knowledge of the true word and bring them under the imperial dominion, I have written very exactly.

Novel or for some persons difficult to believe though the things narrated may be, I assure you they can be accepted without hesitation as strictly factual. Better than to exaggerate, I have minimized all things. It is enough to say that the relation is offered your majesty for truth. I beg that it may be received as homage since it is the most one could bring who returned thence naked.

THE QUEEN: Thank you. Now put on your clothes and get out of here and wipe that blood off our hands.

JOE: Thank you.

OSCAR: Gracias.

AMERICAN THEATER IN LITERATURE (ATL)

Developed by The Contemporary Arts Educational Project, Inc., a nonprofit corporation, and published through its Sun & Moon Press, the American Theater in Literature program was established to promote American theater as a literary form and to educate readers about contemporary and modern theater. The program publishes work of major American playwrights as well as younger, developing dramatists in various publishing program of the Press. The program has also worked with theater companies such as The Mark Taper Forum (Los Angeles), Primary Stages (New York), Soho Rep (New York), Undermain Theatre (Dallas), Bottom's Dream (Los Angeles) and En Garde Arts (New York) to publish plays in connection with their original productions.

BOOKS IN THIS PROGRAM

Robert Auletta *The Persians* ($9.95)
(A Mark Taper Forum Play)

Len Jenkin *Dark Ride and Other Plays* ($13.95)
(Sun & Moon Classics: 22)

Matthew Maguire *The Tower* ($8.95)

Kier Peters *The Confirmation* ($6.95)

Len Jenkin *Careless Love* ($9.95)
(A Soho Rep Play/Sun & Moon Classics: 54)

Mac Wellman *Crowtet 1: A Murder of Crows* and
The Hyacinth Macaw ($11.95)
(Primary Stages Plays/Sun & Moon Classics: 62)

Jeffrey M. Jones *Love Trouble* ($10.95)
(An Undermain Theatre Play/Sun & Moon Classics: 84)

David Greenspan *Son of an Engineer* ($8.95)

Matthew Maguire *Phaedra* ($8.95)

Djuna Barnes *At the Roots of the Stars:
The Short Plays* ($12.95)
(Sun & Moon Classics: 53)

Jeffrey M. Jones and Jonathan Larson
J. P. Morgan Saves the Nation ($9.95)
(An En Garde Arts Play/Sun & Moon Classics: 157)

Mac Wellman *The Land Beyond the Forest:
Dracula* and *Swoop* ($12.95)
(A Soho Rep Play/Sun & Moon Classics: 112)

Erik Ehn *Beginner* ($9.95)
(An Undermain Theatre Book)

Suzan-Lori Parks *Imperceptible Mutabilities
in the Third Kingdom* ($10.95)

John Steppling *Sea of Cortez and Other Plays* ($14.95)
(Sun & Moon Classics: 96)

John Jesurun *Everything That Rises Must Converge* ($11.95)
(Sun & Moon Classics: 116)

OHIO UNIVERSITY LIBRARY

Please return this book as soon as you have finished with it. In order to avoid a fine it must be returned by the latest date stamped below. All books are subject to recall after two weeks or immediately if needed for reserve.